Writing Online and Audio Stories

Guiding readers through the unique challenges and choices presented by digital publication, this book provides a practical set of tools to help students, creatives, and content professionals craft emotionally engaging nonfiction stories for online readers and listeners.

From considering what story to tell, to bringing narratives to life in practice, Anna Faherty explains what gives stories their unique power and demonstrates how to successfully combine techniques from short-stories and screen-writing with journalistic practices like fact checking and verification. Examples from corporate websites, personal blogs, podcasts, and social media set out how to attract and involve readers and listeners, and how to prompt them to take action. Readers will come away with a straightforward framework for planning and crafting storytelling projects and an understanding of text and script development, copyright, and editing. Each chapter includes summaries of key principles and practical writing tips, while case studies share insights from writers' professional practices – including those who use storytelling to influence customers or advocate for change.

Writing Online and Audio Stories is a valuable entry-point for creative writers, podcasters, and professionals in PR and marketing, as well as students undertaking courses such as Digital Writing, Creative Nonfiction and Multimedia Storytelling.

Anna Faherty is an Honorary Lecturer at University College London and an Associate Lecturer at University of the Arts London. Anna also runs the writing, training and content development consultancy Strategic Content. Her clients include The Design Museum, Natural History Museum, Wellcome Collection and V&A.

T0384888

Writing Online and Audio Stories

Crafting Nonfiction for Websites, Podcasts, and Social Media

Anna Faherty

Routledge
Taylor & Francis Group

NEW YORK AND LONDON

Designed cover image: © Getty Images

First published 2024
by Routledge
605 Third Avenue, New York, NY 10158

and by Routledge
4 Park Square, Milton Park, Abingdon, Oxon, OX14 4RN

*Routledge is an imprint of the Taylor & Francis Group,
an informa business*

Library of Congress Cataloging-in-Publication Data
Names: Faherty, Anna, author.
Title: Writing online and audio stories : crafting nonfiction for websites,
podcasts, and social media / Anna Faherty.
Description: New York : Routledge, 2023. | Includes bibliographical
references and index.
Identifiers: LCCN 2023032201 (print) | LCCN 2023032202 (ebook) | ISBN
9781032425856 (hardback) | ISBN 9781032425849 (paperback) | ISBN
9781003363347 (ebook)
Subjects: LCSH: Online authorship. | Social media--Authorship. | Digital
media.
Classification: LCC PN171.O55 F34 2023 (print) | LCC PN171.O55 (ebook) |
DDC 808/.042--dc23/eng/20230824
LC record available at https://lccn.loc.gov/2023032201
LC ebook record available at https://lccn.loc.gov/2023032202

ISBN: 9781032425856 (hbk)
ISBN: 9781032425849 (pbk)
ISBN: 9781003363347 (ebk)

DOI: 10.4324/9781003363347

Typeset in Galliard
by KnowledgeWorks Global Ltd.

For Carol. Shame you couldn't edit it.

Contents

Acknowledgements

My thanks to …

Danny Birchall, who initiated me into the adventure of digital storytelling and enabled me to research it from an academic perspective.

Judith Watts – always a delight and an inspiration. And a committed and constructive first reader.

Ed Paleit and Pete Goodman, without whom I'd never have taught the course at City University that forms the spine of this book. And all the multimedia storytelling students I taught there – who taught me as much about structure and style as I hope I taught them.

Wendy Sugarman – for support, love and understanding, and your expertise on lived experience and inclusion.

Numerous friends and contacts provided insightful and encouraging feedback on concepts and drafts, including Laura Smith, Nadia Al Yafai, Sally Annett, Zoe Jacobs, Kirsty Hunter, Clare Hodder, Kate Brewin, Jon Reed, and Simon Coppock. Richard Gerrig, Melanie Grant, and Tom van Lauer each provided swift and helpful guidance during my construction of the Story Funnel, though any criticisms of the model should be aimed squarely at me.

Writers who generously allowed me to share their work and/or talked about their process, along with those who helped formalise permissions agreements: Lauren Abramo (Dystel, Goderich & Bourret), Art Institute of Chicago, Yarrie Bangura (Aunty's Ginger Tonic), Allison Behringer (*Bodies* podcast), Chris Berube (*99% Invisible*), Bonner Private Research, Rachel Bruce, Mukti Jain Campion, Brooke Chang, Lara Chapple (Novel), Beth Collier (Curious Minds), Lori Cuthbert (*National Geographic*), Augusta Declan, Jacqueline Dooley, Douglas Fox, Amber Garvey (United Agents), Rebecca Groves (The Nocturnists), Dan Gugler (KornFerry), Ariane Judet (Oxfam GB), Evan Krask (WME), King Kurus (*Black History Buff*), Alexandra Lange (*99% Invisible*), Helen Molesworth, Jenna Molster (NPR), Ijeoma Oluo, Ben Percy, Madhuraa Prakash, Ash Rathod, Electra Rhodes, Josh Robbins, Dani Shapiro, Emily Silverman (The Nocturnists), Jahlila Stamp (Curtis Brown), Olivia Stroud (V&A), Michon Vanderpoel (Rebel Girls, Inc.), Roy Wadia (WHO), Kitty Whitehead (Smithsonian). Apologies to anyone I have inadvertently overlooked. Mea culpa.

About this book

In a world where everyone vies for our time online, nonfiction stories are powerful tools for gaining attention, connecting with others, and driving change. This practical book supports you through the process of shaping, writing, and publishing short-form nonfiction stories that will be distributed online.

Stories like this may be found on social media (particularly on Twitter/X and LinkedIn), on blogs and websites (like corporate "About us" pages or crowdsourcing pitches), and in podcasts. Whether you're telling stories about your pathway to leadership, your experience of living with a health condition, or because you want to advocate for change, this book is for you.

The concept for the book grew out of a popular second-year undergraduate course on multimedia storytelling which I taught for several years at City University, London. Hosted by the School of English, the module was offered to students from departments as diverse as sociology, criminology, and music production. Frustratingly, I was never able to find a suitable book to serve as a core text for this module, so I decided to write one.

What is "online storytelling"?

I've called this book *Writing Online and Audio Stories* in an attempt to distinguish it from texts on "digital storytelling". I might just as well have called it "Writing digital stories", but books on digital stories often focus on visual or video storytelling. This book, on the other hand, is dedicated solely to *stories told in words* – words which might be heard or read.

On one level, online storytelling has much in common with writing for print. Writers in both media must recreate what writing coach Jack Hart calls "the lush, palpable stuff of human existence" with words alone.[1] Yet book writers have the privilege of writing at length, for people willing and able to devote time to reading. Throughout, this book assumes you're writing short-form pieces – stories of no more than 2,000 words, and often far fewer. When writing for websites or social media, gaining and maintaining attention is a formidable challenge. Online writers must get straight to the point, adopt an intimate tone, and structure their writing in short, focused scenes.

Who is this book for?

This book provides a practical set of tools to help anyone craft emotionally involving nonfiction stories for online and audio publication. From considering what stories to tell, to bringing them to life in practice, the book demonstrates the impact of stories, while sharing examples and advice to help you get started with online nonfiction storytelling.

Within higher education, the text should appeal to creative writing students (taking modules like "creative nonfiction", "digital writing" or "digital storytelling"), marketing students (on "content marketing" and "PR" modules), and journalism and publishing students (taking "digital", "feature-writing", or "content" modules). It will be useful for content designers and other creative professionals, too, including marketing and PR staff who need to understand and apply the mechanics of online story construction.

The content is relevant to anyone who writes in English. The case studies and examples of published writing are sourced from Australia, Canada, Kenya, Nigeria, UK, and US.

What will you gain by reading this book?

What sets this book apart from general storytelling guides or marketing texts is the focus on how to write nonfiction stories for online publication. It is not a book about how to build your brand, source more followers or sell more stuff (though you will learn something about how people do these things). It's a book that teaches you how to write the *stories* that allow you to build a brand, gather followers, or sell things.

While the book includes examples of storytelling for websites, blogs, podcasts, and social media, the emphasis is on writing and scripting for these media, rather than choosing appropriate channels or the technical production of multimedia content. These aspects are, of course, well-covered elsewhere. Throughout, I draw inspiration from the processes and tools used by short-story writers and screenwriters, since these forms share some of the key constraints of online content: needing to hook the reader early on and keeping things short. Key journalistic practices, like fact checking and verification, are also included.

As a writer, I hope you'll find this an easy and enjoyable read – because if it's not enjoyable, you may give up before you encounter anything useful. If you stick around, you should gain a number of benefits.

- An understanding of the power of story, based on research around how and why stories impact readers and listeners.
- A straightforward framework of six ingredients, which may be mixed together to create any story.
- Practical tips for crafting copy that builds connections, enables readers and listeners to construct their own stories, and transports them into the action.

- Professional insights into the nitty-gritty of audience research, story planning, fact checking, copyright clearance, and editing.
- An appreciation that stories perpetuate or challenge societal norms, along with guidelines for inclusive writing.
- An understanding of how writing for listeners differs from writing for readers.

Reading this book should help you appreciate the challenges, techniques, and value of writing online nonfiction. However, reading a book will not transform you into a writer. If you apply the principles in practice, you'll learn something. You'll gain even more if you apply and adapt them over and over again. As the subtitle to this book highlights, writing is a craft. It's a skill that people who call themselves writers develop over time; a skill you hone each and every time you write. By all means soak up the advice shared in this book, and in the excellent publications that I've suggested as further reading. But augment that by reading and listening to other writers' work, by writing as much and as often as you can, and by seeking feedback on what you write.

What's inside?

The book comprises eight chapters split into two parts. While you may read the parts – and indeed the chapters – in any order, the whole has been constructed to take you on a journey from understanding online audiences to the practical craft of online storytelling and writing. Each chapter builds on the one before. If you read the book from front to back, you'll build your knowledge and skills step by step.

Part I Understanding audiences and stories
1 Understanding online readers and listeners
2 How we respond to stories: the Story Funnel
3 Six essential story ingredients

Part II Developing online and audio stories
4 Storytelling with purpose
5 Constructing your story
6 Telling your story
7 Writing for listeners
8 Reviewing, editing, and publishing your story

Part I Understanding audiences and stories

Chapters 1 and 2 provide the contextual foundation for the book. They consider the nature of online audiences before demonstrating how stories impact readers and listeners, by way of a new theoretical model: the Story Funnel. Examples are drawn from global news organisations and individuals who use stories to connect with others. Armed with this knowledge, Chapter 3 introduces the six ingredients required to construct any story. Extracts from published online stories and podcasts illustrate how these principles are applied in practice, while consideration is given to whether AI story programs will ever replace writers.

Part II Developing online and audio stories

Chapter 4 explores the importance of purpose and author brand, while considering the challenges and rewards of telling your own story. It helps you define why you're writing, so you can make appropriate choices as you work. Examples come from individuals, charities, and brands who tell stories online, including those who use stories – and public narrative – to advocate for change.

Chapters 5 and 6 focus on the practicalities of shaping and writing nonfiction stories for online and audio. They cover finding an angle, plotting your story and developing a story outline, before sharing detailed guidance around writing. The concept of inclusive writing is introduced.

Chapter 7 addresses the specific context of audio storytelling. Drawing on examples from a range of podcasts, it considers the unique needs of listeners, the use of interview "tape", and the role of an audio script.

Chapter 8 focuses on one of the most important parts of the writing process: revising and editing your work. It includes practical guidance on fact checking and copyright clearance, while highlighting the need to take care of readers and listeners, sources, and yourself.

Each chapter includes examples of online nonfiction storytelling in practice, an end-of-chapter summary (with lessons for online writers), and key reading recommendations.

Note

1 Jack Hart, *The Complete Guide to Writing Narrative Nonfiction* (Chicago: University of Chicago Press, 2011)

Part I

Understanding audiences and stories

1 Understanding online readers and listeners

This introductory chapter explores the needs and wants of people who read or listen online. Drawing inspiration from research conducted by major news organisations, it provides practical tools to help you get to know your own specific readers or listeners. The chapter covers:

- How readers and listeners behave
- Why people read and listen online
- What online readers and listeners want
- How to research your own audience
- Developing and using empathy

When I write for online and audio, I picture my readers and listeners as wild animals. To be precise, I see them as hungry leopards, mouths agape, prowling across the African savannah. On the hunt for a belly-filling meal, they lack the energy to chase everything that catches their attention. If they pick up a scent, they decide in a split-second whether to pursue it or move on in search of an easier, tastier kill.[1]

This isn't the image I'd *like* to have in my mind. When I introduce this issue to clients and students, I usually start with a very different picture in my slide deck. It's a photograph of Hollywood actor Gregory Peck, taken some time in the 1960s – a lush Technicolor shot that wouldn't look out of place in the TV show *Mad Men*.

In the photo, Gregory sits comfortably in what appears to be his living room. He holds an open book in one hand, a pipe in the other. His eyes are fixed on the page before him; he looks lost in a story. Like any writer, I'd love my readers and listeners to be just like Gregory – people who have time to sit back, put their feet up, switch off distractions, and immerse themselves in my ripping yarns, people who choose to spend time with me, eager to gain a return on the investment they've made in my words.

DOI: 10.4324/9781003363347-2

Figure 1.1 Offline vs online readers: immersed and attentive vs scanning and hungry

Book readers, theatre audiences, and cinema-goers *do* have something in common with Gregory. They've made a decision to invest time and money in whatever comes their way. They usually stick with the story until the end, unless something untoward upsets their reading or listening experience. On the Internet, readers and listeners are very different beasts, as Figure 1.1 highlights. This chapter explains why, while sharing advice on how to get under the skin of your own readers and listeners.

Why your audience matters

Online, it's incredibly easy to publish anything you want. Whack out some words, paste or upload them onto a ready-made platform, and hit publish without giving your reader or listener a second thought. But if you want to increase the odds of your words being read or listened to – and of them having any impact – getting to know your audience is key.

Here are just a few reasons why it's worth taking time to understand readers and listeners.

1 **It's common sense.** Would you start to cook a meal for someone without checking their dietary preferences? What if you were organising a party or compiling a playlist – wouldn't you want to know what people like or dislike, what excites them and what turns them off? Writing's the same. If you

know your audience, you and your stories are more likely to click with readers or listeners.

2 **You understand the rules of the game.** Sitting in a garret, writing for your own amusement, is all very well, but if you want people to read or listen to your words, you need to work within certain parameters. If you know what works online (and what doesn't) you'll write stories that people might actually want to spend time with.

3 **You'll create relevant stories.** If you know what interests your audience, what they already know, and what they care about, your stories will resonate. As we'll see in Chapter 2, the more familiar a reader or listener is with the topic of a story, the more likely they are to lose themselves within it. If you want your audience to stick with you past your first few lines, you need to know what feels familiar to them.

4 **You can tailor your language and tone.** Writing is all about choices. Once you've decided what story to tell, you'll make countless decisions about how to tell it. Knowing something about how your audience speaks and how they connect with one another online will help you write in an appropriate style. When it comes to making decisions about individual words and phrases, this knowledge means you'll make clear, accessible, inclusive choices.

5 **You can build a following.** If you know from the outset who you're writing for, you can be strategic about what stories you write and how you market them. Over time, you'll build a brand by telling stories that resonate and sharing them with people who'll be interested.

Luckily, there are plenty of people who have already completed audience research for you, so the first half of this chapter shares some of the most useful findings from other people's studies. Once you've absorbed this, go a step further, because the more you know about *your* specific audience, the better writing choices you'll make. You might talk to the people you're writing for, complete a full-on reader survey, or conduct empathic thought experiments. The second half of this chapter provides tips and tools for each of these strategies.

A distracting environment

Online readers and listeners are far more fickle than offline readers like Gregory Peck. Online readers don't sit still and they won't just read or listen to whatever comes their way. They choose how to spend their time. They have "agency": the power to play an active role in the media they consume.

Online, they have any number of alternative content options just a click, swipe, or alt-tab away. The founder of Nieman Lab, a project exploring how journalism works in the Internet age, puts it well when he explains: "your attention is literally up for auction hundreds or thousands of times a day".[2] Like readers and listeners, online platforms have agency too; their algorithms monitor our online behaviour, controlling what we all see.[2]

In practice, this leads to sobering statistics, like those shared in *Slate* magazine by tech columnist Farhad Manjoo.[3]

- If 100 people land on your story, about 38 will click away immediately.
- Another 3 will stop when forced to scroll.
- Around 28 will disappear before they've made it halfway through.
- You'll lose another 6 before the next forced scroll.

Do the maths and you're left with just 25 people (out of 100) who scroll through two screens-worth of your story. In short: even when your marketing efforts lead people to your story, you lose most of them. The majority switch their attention away before they reach the halfway point.

For anyone who sticks with Manjoo's article, the journalist explains what's behind these statistics. "I want to finish the whole thing, I really do", says Manjoo. "I wish you would, too … But, who am I kidding. I'm busy. You're busy. There's always something else to read, watch, play, or eat."

Sometimes distractions can come not from other websites, but from the content itself. In a study conducted by Nielsen Norman Group, researchers found that on-page features like displayed quotes or ads disrupted reading. Readers who initially consumed every word switched to "scanning" – a less immersive reading style more suited to spotting and extracting information.[4]

Though online listeners tend to be more engaged than online readers, they're often working or studying, driving or travelling, walking, exercising, or completing household chores, all while tuned in. Even when they want to listen intently, they may not be able to. As popular Irish broadcaster Sir Terry Wogan said about his radio audience, "They're only half-listening. They're walking in and out of the kitchen or they're in the car … It's a mistake to think that everybody's clinging to your every word."[5]

Satisfying online readers and listeners therefore relies on gaining their attention – not just at the start, but all the way to the end. Fail to maintain interest and they'll click away, just like a hungry leopard moving on to a more appetising kill. However much I wish otherwise, I've known for a long time that:

Online
Readers
Are
Not
Like
Gregory.

Why people read and listen online

Given these challenges, you might wonder why you'd bother to write stories for online readers and listeners in the first place. After all, isn't everyone just streaming video these days? Yes, video *is* hugely popular, but people still read stories online and people listen to story-based podcasts. While statistics around media use change every year, there are lasting reasons why audiences continue to choose to read or listen in online formats.

1 **Choice and personalisation.** Online readers and podcast listeners value the ability to control what they access, when, and where.
2 **Access and pace.** Compared with video, it's easier and quicker to find and access information when it's presented as text. Readers aren't forced to sit through pre-start ads and they have more control of how they absorb information. They may pause and reflect, glance, or scroll back. They work through everything at their own, preferred pace.
3 **Interest and credibility.** Though scanning is a common online behaviour, people *will* read articles in more depth if the content reflects their experience and concerns. Similarly, listeners seek out trusted voices with shared interests.[6]
4 **Multitasking.** Online readers may consume other content on other devices as they read. Podcast listeners go one better: they use their ears and brains to expand their worlds while their eyes and hands are otherwise engaged.
5 **Avoiding visual stimulation.** Podcasts offer welcome escape from overstimulating screen time. Audio formats help people incorporate stories into their time-poor, media-saturated lives without the need to stare at another screen.[7]

Each of these points is, of course, a generalisation that treats readers and listeners as an anonymous mass of people. Yet one of the key principles I always follow is that readers and listeners are individuals. As Nicole Fenton and Kate Kiefer Lee point out in their excellent book, *Nicely Said: Writing for the Web with Style and Purpose,* anyone producing content for the web should remember that they're writing for real people, who have feelings, needs, and busy lives.[8]

Any audience comprises people with diverse backgrounds and priorities, people interested in different things, people with specific worries and needs. When you think of your audience as a cluster of unique individuals rather than an abstract mass, it prompts two useful reflections.

1 **Everyone has their own preference about the type of media they want to consume and when**. For instance, people who instinctively think in pictures have an inbuilt ability to conjure up images from a textual description. For them, video adds little to a well-told story.[9] People who don't think in pictures, however, may choose to watch video or other visual stories.
2 **Everyone has a different reason for reading or listening.** Writers therefore need to know who their own audience is and what makes them tick.

What online readers and listeners want

Sometimes audience needs are obvious. For instance, if someone's searching for information about when a celebrity was born or how to unclog a blocked drain, they want a quick and clear answer that solves their problem. But sometimes people have more contextual and emotional needs, as research by the BBC World Service highlights.

In practice: BBC World Service user needs

The BBC World Service delivers news around the globe in 41 languages. While many news organisations focus on updating audiences with the latest information, the World Service takes on a different role. Because most World Service users see or hear the headlines via other, local news reports, they come to the BBC looking for something else.

To explore what users were looking for, the BBC researched what its audiences said about the World Service. The results identified six categories of needs, all articulated from the user perspective:

- Update me
- Give me perspective
- Educate me
- Keep me on trend
- Amuse me
- Inspire me

Two of these ("update me" and "give me perspective") are satisfied by regular news bulletins and analyses, which the BBC has always delivered. Needs like "inspire me", though, aren't typically satisfied by newsrooms. Effective "inspire me" content is likely to be long form, with a structure more commonly seen in fiction. This might be, for instance, a story of an individual achieving something against the odds.

At a strategic level, this research exercise enabled the BBC to develop new types of content to satisfy the full range of user needs. On a smaller scale, Digital Development Editor Dmitry Shishkin views the needs as prompts that can help individual writers develop interesting, sharable content, able to stand out in a crowded online space.[10]

The BBC's six user needs apply equally well to online content that has nothing to do with news. For instance, podcast users are also motivated by information, education, entertainment, and inspiration. These motivations depend on where someone is when they listen. Out-of-home users tend towards entertainment and inspiration; in-home listeners focus on information-seeking.

Being a friend

One need not highlighted in the BBC research is the need for connection, something that listeners particularly value. While the intimate atmosphere of podcasts enables listeners to build relationships with hosts, one survey showed that 83 per cent of listeners viewed their favourite podcasters as friends.[11]

Though reading may not foster the same atmosphere, an online writer's words often end up cradled in readers' hands. If read on a mobile phone, they're stroked and swiped, squeezed into pockets and laid to rest on pillows, never far from reach. This makes reading on mobile a far more intimate experience than reading on a computer or listening to a radio.

Overall, the Internet is, says journalist and academic Rosalind Coward, a place where, "the usual social barriers ... seem to be lowered". For Coward, the Internet and social media are quintessentially personal spaces. In these worlds of "direct unmediated communication", online audiences expect access to stories of triumph over tragedy, told as if related by a friend.[12]

Though broad-based user needs like these provide useful checklists and handy starting points for ways into stories, in practice, audience needs are more fluid and specific. My online readers-as-leopards analogy is therefore limited. It highlights the need to grab and maintain attention, without considering the myriad reasons why an individual reader or listener may be interested (or not) in what you're saying. The only way to do that is by getting to know your audience.

Getting to know your specific audience

American psychologist Steven Pinker describes writing as "an act of pretence", because the person you're communicating with isn't present.[13] You can't see, watch, or extract feedback from your reader or listener – at least not in real time. And they can't interrupt or ask for clarification while you're writing. In some ways, a writer's job isn't too far removed from what a small child does when they talk to an imaginary friend.

The simplest way to gain a rich understanding of your audience is to put your imagination to work and picture them in your mind. Many writers have a clear image of what this imagined friend is like. Freelance audio producer Karen Pearlman imagines her listener as a commuter stuck in traffic on a gridlocked freeway. Writer Antonio Tabucchi imagines he's writing for someone open to the world and the randomness of life, while journalist Don Murray's imagined reader stands by his side, blurting out questions, which Murray dutifully answers.[14]

To picture your imagined reader or listener, first think about *who* they are. Then pose the following questions.

- Where are they as they read or listen?
- What are they doing?
- What's their relationship to you?
- What do they want to know?
- What do they care about?

Researching your audience

Developing your own imagined reader or listener is a useful exercise, but it's all the more effective if your imaginings are based on hard evidence. Big brands and global publishers are, of course, able to invest serious money in researching their audiences, as demonstrated by the *Financial Times (FT)* reader survey, which reached thousands of people.

In practice: the *FT* Reader Survey

The *Financial Times* (*FT*) publishes more than 40 email newsletters, each delivering respected journalism direct to readers' in-boxes. With over 1 million paying subscribers, the *FT* rarely struggles to find online readers, but newsletters add value for the newspaper by creating opportunities to build closer, direct relationships with subscribers.

Like any digital publisher, when the *FT* wants to know about its readers, it collects and analyses data. For newsletters, this data includes subscription levels, email-open rates and clickthrough rates.[15] Yet none of these say much about what readers *care* about. So, when the *FT* wanted to understand what readers enjoyed and what might be improved, they simply asked them.

The *FT* used its own newsletters as a conduit to its readers, adding a brief question at the foot of each newsletter ("How satisfied are you with [newsletter name]?"). Each of the five options (1 (very dissatisfied) to 5 (very satisfied)) led to a detailed survey about the reasons for the given score.

Findings

Some survey responses confirmed the newsletter team's suspicions (for instance, that readers enjoy personality-driven newsletters), while others debunked them. The data encouraged the *FT* to shorten some newsletters and enhance clarity in others. More usefully, the newsletters team aligned the content and form of each newsletter with the reasons readers gave for subscribing. For instance, if readers were attracted by an individual writer, that journalist was encouraged to write longer pieces and reveal more of their personality. If readers valued gaining information at speed, the team focused more on concision.

Here are some of the benefits that this research delivered.

1 **More satisfied readers.** Knowing more about reader satisfaction and what readers value enabled the *FT* to tailor newsletters to drive greater engagement.
2 **Additional revenue and adjacent sales.** Since engaged readers are more likely to convert to and retain a Premium-rate subscription, increased engagement leads to increased revenue.
3 **Strong bonds.** By participating in the survey, sharing their views, and seeing changes driven by their feedback, readers built an even stronger relationship with the *FT*.[16]

If you don't have the budget of the BBC or the *FT*, the cheapest way to conduct audience research is simply to be part of the audience yourself. As an example, the podcast that I co-produce is designed for people with a nerdy interest in what goes on behind the scenes in book publishing. Who better to target than publishers themselves? It works for my co-host, Judith Watts, and me because a) we've spent most of our careers working in or with publishers and b) we spend time in the spaces where publishers spend *their* time, both on- and offline. We're lucky enough to have personal relationships with people in our target audience, so we talk to them about the podcast, discover what works for them, and find out how they'd like to see it develop in the future. This experience reinforces the commonly cited "write what you know" piece of writing advice, since you'll possess (or be able to access) useful knowledge about your audience.

If you aren't already part of your audience, make an effort to spend time where they spend time. Observe what they say and do. Follow who they follow on social media. Get to know them and what matters to them. Ask questions about their lives and priorities. Find out what they read or listen to (and why) and what else they'd like to see. Read or listen to the stories they consume, so you can learn what works for them. You may even want to schedule interviews to speak with readers and listeners in greater depth.

In practice: conducting a research interview

Writers and editors Nicole Fenton and Kate Kiefer Lee value interviews as a useful tool for identifying what readers want to achieve and what stands in their way. Here are four of their excellent tips for running an effective reader interview.

1 **Prepare.** Think through what you want to know and choose a format that's most likely to provide answers to your questions.
2 **Ask neutral, open questions.** Don't lead the other person. Give them space to answer at length. Encourage people to expand on their thoughts by avoiding questions that might be answered with a simple "yes" or "no".
3 **Be conversational.** Listen to what the other person says, allow pauses, and be flexible. If you're working from a list of pre-prepared questions, use these as a guide not a script.
4 **Explain next steps.** At the end, thank the person for their time and explain where their input fits into your writing. Allow them to ask questions of you too.[17]

Even when you do speak directly to readers or listeners, they may not be aware of their underlying needs and wants. Think about those times when you unthinkingly pick up your phone and start browsing. You probably need some form of relief from a dull, out-of-control, or stressful day, though you may not consciously know it. When people don't consciously know what they want, writers must delve into readers' or listeners' inner worlds to deduce what's going on. To do this, you'll need to put yourself in a reader or listener's shoes.

Putting yourself in their shoes

If you have some basic knowledge of who your reader or listener is, and a picture of them in your mind, you're ready to step into their shoes and imagine what it's like to be them. Think about what's going on in their life, what's on their mind, and any unspoken needs they may have. Try to identify *direct* content needs (like "I want to read something inspirational" or "I want to listen to a true-crime story") and *adjacent* life needs (like "I want to feel less isolated" or "I wish I knew more about what's going on in the world").

Never underestimate the importance of understanding what's going on in the world around your readers or listeners too. I find YouGov (yougov.co.uk) and the Pew Research Center (pewresearch.org) excellent resources for this. Freely accessible online, both websites publish information about what people think and how they behave. Ever wondered how people rate their political leaders and the prevailing view about a woman's right to abortion? What about people's favourite drinks and how often they change their bedsheets? You'll find answers on these sites. I search each for data on specific topics or browse to step outside my own personal bubble. They provide an Aladdin's Cave of audience insights – treasure that improves your understanding of other people, while also leading you towards unexpected story ideas.

Putting yourself in someone else's shoes is, of course, a way to see the world from someone else's perspective. If you're able to do this easily, you already have the storyteller's superpower: empathy. If this perspective-taking doesn't come naturally, don't panic. There are practical steps you can take to develop your empathic powers.

Understanding and developing empathy

Empathy is the ability to understand someone else's feelings and perspective. Writer Rebecca Solnit views empathy as an *active practice* of "paying attention to other people" to help us understand a world beyond our own.[18] Empathy ensures that good writers don't just babble on without considering their audience; empathy makes a well-planned piece of writing feel like a natural conversation.

I think of empathy as a storytelling superpower because it sits at the heart of two important aspects of writing. Empathic people tend to make good storytellers for two reasons.

1 **They understand the audience perspective.** Because empathic people anticipate how their words will be received and interpreted, they frame their writing for best effect. They choose appropriate words, gauge which aspects need to be explained in depth, and appreciate those they can skip over.

2 **They understand the story perspective.** Empathic people are able to put themselves in the shoes of the people they write about. They imagine what it would be like to experience a story from the perspective of the people within it.

In his book *Empathy: A Handbook for Revolution* public philosopher Roman Krznaric shares five easy activities you can try out to enhance your empathy skills.[19]

1 **Imagine yourself in someone else's life.** Spend time thinking about what another person's life is like: how they think, behave, and feel. In a writing context, think about where your audience is when they read or listen to your words, what they're doing and what else might be on their mind.
2 **Be curious about strangers.** Talk to people you don't know and ask questions – though take care not to be intrusive or interrogative. Krznaric suggests scheduling time in your diary to talk to a stranger once a week. While opening your mind to other people's experiences, talking to strangers may also lead to unexpected story ideas.
3 **Whenever you listen to someone, consciously consider their perspective.** Look behind their words to consider what they may be feeling and needing. Don't take everything at face value. Ask yourself why they speak or behave in a certain way.
4 **Don't just talk to people, live their lives.** Job swap with someone for a day, or shadow someone in their everyday life. This helps you to appreciate what other people's lives are really like, what difficulties people face, and what unmet needs they may have. And it's another fantastic way to find new stories.
5 **Engage in 'armchair travel'.** Read books, listen to podcasts, and watch movies to expose yourself to other cultures, behaviours, and perspectives. The more you open your world to different ways of thinking, the more you'll consider different perspectives on that world.

Empathy mapping

Empathy mapping is a tool that helps you to organise what you know about what's going on in someone else's world. By focusing your attention on their feelings, wants, and hopes, empathy mapping helps you appreciate how your writing fits into their life and – ideally – adds value to it.

Empathy mapping involves:

1 Defining who you are mapping.
2 Exploring the sorts of things they think, see, do, say, and hear.
3 Identifying their key fears, frustrations, needs, and hopes (effectively imagining what it *feels* like to be them).

While it may seem counterintuitive to focus on one person, particularly if you're expecting your work to be seen or heard by hundreds or thousands of people, this process helps you home in on the key aspects that matter to your *ideal* reader or listener.

There are plenty of online templates for gathering and presenting this information, but they all look a little like the example in Figure 1.2.

Figure 1.2 An empathy map template

In practice: make an empathy map

1 *Set up a template*
Sketch out a template based on Figure 1.2 or download one from the web.[20]
2 *Name and describe*
Before you do anything else, decide who your ideal reader or listener is, place them in the centre and give them a name. A name helps bring them to life so you think about one individual rather than an amorphous, abstract "audience".

Identify as much descriptive information about this individual as you can. Ask yourself questions like: How old are they? Where do they live? What's their relationship status? What's their job? How do they relax? Who do they spend time with? What do they enjoy doing?
3 *Step into their shoes*
Work your way around the four prompts. These are designed to get you thinking deeply about the major influences on your ideal reader or listener's life.

a **What are they thinking and feeling?**
What makes them feel good? What keeps them up at night? What's uppermost in their mind right now?
b **What do they see other people doing?**
In their immediate environment. On social media. What else are they reading?
c **What do they hear other people talking about?**
How does this make them feel? How does it influence them? What else do they listen to?

d **What do they say and do?**

Sum up what's going on with them in one sentence. Are their words and actions ever contradictory? Why might that be?

Don't worry if you find it difficult to answer some of these questions – that's normal. Look back at all your research and dig deeper by asking "why?" For instance, if you know your reader wants to stay up to date with current affairs, drill down to work out why this might be. Is it a practical need related to their job, a personal preference, or a sign that they care about how others view them? If you're not sure, can you ask them?

4 *Identify pains and gains*

Your ultimate aim is to identify two or three "gains" (goals that your audience member wants to achieve in order to improve their life) and two or three "pains" (the obstacles that prevent them achieving these goals). You can then select and construct stories that help them achieve these goals.

5 *Draw valuable insights*

Finally, consider the consequences for your writing. For instance, if a reader is always super-busy, you'll need to be short and sweet. If a listener loves getting under the skin of people, you'll need to provide enough depth to allow them to do so. If someone always feels like they're behind the curve, you'll need to develop new, cutting-edge content.

If you struggle with identifying fundamental needs, you might like to raid Seth Godin's list of universal dreams and fears. In his book *This is Marketing,* Godin points out that, while everyone on the planet is a unique individual, we're all fundamentally driven by similar emotional needs.[21] Godin lists 32 of these needs, though you could add plenty more. For now, here are ten, which should provide some food for thought.

Adventure	Nostalgia
Belonging	Peace of mind
Control	Power
Delight	Strength
Freedom of movement	Tension

Choosing from a list of needs, or scribbling in sections of an empathy map, can sometimes feel a bit like you're just making things up. If you're completing this exercise to spark story ideas, then that doesn't matter – because you're more interested in stimulating your imagination than revealing a deeper truth. However, if you're constructing an empathy map so your writing aligns with proven reader or listener needs, it ought to be as accurate as possible.

To improve accuracy, draw on all the knowledge you already have about your readers or listeners – recall conversations that you've had with them, things that you've seen them do, and challenges that you know some of them experience. Incorporate wider research (like the information shared in the first half of this chapter) and look beyond what they do and say to decode what they're thinking and feeling.

Once you've identified your audience and their needs, keep your notes and empathy map close to hand. Print them out and stick them somewhere you can see while you write. They'll serve as a useful reminder of who you're writing for and what matters to them. An alternative way to articulate the needs you've identified is in the form of reader or listener stories.

Reader and listener stories

Like the user stories produced by web developers and content designers, reader and listener stories are one-sentence statements that summarise who you're writing for and what they need. Written from the reader or listener perspective, they follow this format:

As a (blah), I want to (blah), so I can (blah)

For instance, you might construct a user story that says something like,

> **As a** socially conscious millennial, **I want to** discover new perspectives on news stories, **so I can** discuss and debate current affairs with my friends.

or

> **As a** time-poor working mum, **I want to** read light, uplifting stories, **so I can** escape from the stresses of my busy life.

Don't worry if these statements feel a bit clunky – they're not designed to be published to the wider world. They summarise a fundamental truth about your audience for *you*, a truth that points you in a specific writing direction. Along with any other research insights. keep these stories close to hand, so they remain top of mind as you write. They'll help you to sense-check story ideas and angles, influence style and word choices, and write with your reader or listener in mind.

Overall, online readers and listeners want to be entertained, educated, or inspired. They appreciate interesting topics and human connection. And, if they want to keep external distractions at bay, they need to become absorbed and involved in the content they're consuming. What's the best format to deliver all that? A story. If you want your readers to be less like leopards and more like Gregory, stories are the only answer. In the next chapter we'll find out why.

Summary

- Online audiences consume content for many different reasons, including updating themselves, providing perspective, keeping on trend, education, amusement, or inspiration. They appreciate choosing what they read or listen to and how and when they do so.
- Online readers are highly likely to click away at the very start of your story. They may be distracted by the world around them or interruptions within the story itself.
- Online listeners are probably multitasking, so can't give full attention to a story.
- Neither readers nor listeners are able to interrupt and ask for clarification. This makes writing akin to chatting to an imaginary friend.
- Particularly if mediated through a mobile phone, the relationship with your reader or listener is an intimate one.
- Online readers and listeners want inspirational content that entertains and interests them, delivered in a strong voice.

Practical lessons for online writers

- **Get to know your readers and listeners.** Talk to them, gather information about them, imagine what it's like to be them. Use tools like empathy mapping and reader and listener stories to collate and display your findings.
- **Look beyond what readers and listeners say.** Identify underlying needs and motivations, what they're interested in, and their fundamental pains and gains.
- **Use your findings as you plan and write.** Select and develop stories that support your audience to achieve their goals. Write in a style that works for them.
- **Grab and maintain attention.** Craft titles, introductory content, and first lines to pull readers and listeners in. Keep your story tight and your writing concise, focused, and relevant. Be direct, straightforward, and unambiguous.
- **Create an intimate experience.** Treat your reader or listener like a friend. Be open and vulnerable. Write in a conversational tone.
- **Focus on interest and inspiration.** Choose to write stories that fit into your reader's or listener's world. Write about relevant topics and inspirational people.

Recommended reading

Nicole Fenton and Kate Kiefer Lee, *Nicely Said: Writing for the Web with Style and Purpose* (Berkeley, CA: Peachpit Press, 2014) – chapter 2, "Get Your Bearings", provides helpful guidance about knowing your readers.

Notes and references

1 This way of thinking about readers was inspired by Henneke Duistermaat's description of readers as panthers, available here: <https://www.enchantingmarketing.com/writing-for-the-web-vs-print/>

2 Joshua Benton, "What's the Best Way to Deal with a Flood of Misinformation? Maybe it's Time for Some Deliberate Ignorance", Nieman Lab, 15 November 2022 <https://www.niemanlab.org/2022/11/whats-the-best-way-to-deal-with-a-flood-of-misinformation-maybe-its-time-for-some-deliberate-ignorance/> (accessed 24 November 2022)

3 Farhad Manjoo, "You Won't Finish This Article", *Slate*, 6 June 2013 <https://slate.com/technology/2013/06/how-people-read-online-why-you-wont-finish-this-article.html> (accessed 14 December 2022)

4 Kate Moran, "How People Read Online: New and Old Findings", Nielsen Norman Group, 5 April 2020 <https://www.nngroup.com/articles/how-people-read-online/> (accessed 14 December 2022)

5 BBC Sounds, *Desert Island Discs: Sir Terry Wogan*, 1 January 2012 <https://www.bbc.co.uk/sounds/play/b018w7rj> (accessed 14 December 2022)

6 Nir Grinberg, "Identifying Modes of User Engagement with Online News and Their Relationship to Information Gain in Text", in *WWW 2018: The 2018 Web Conference, April 23–27, 2018, Lyon, France* (ACM: New York, 2018) <https://doi.org/10.1145/3178876.3186180>; Nielsen, *Podcasts are Resonating with Diverse Audiences*, 2021 <https://www.nielsen.com/insights/2021/podcasts-are-resonating-with-diverse-audiences> (accessed 2 January 2023)

7 Spotify Advertising, *Sonic Science: Understanding Your Brain on Sound*, 2022 <https://ads.spotify.com/en-GB/news-and-insights/sonic-science> (accessed 15 December 2022)

8 Nicole Fenton and Kate Kiefer Lee, *Nicely Said: Writing for the Web with Style and Purpose* (Berkeley, CA: Peachpit Press, 2014)

9 Nic Newman, "Overview and Key Findings of the 2022 Digital News Report", Reuters Institute, 2022 <https://reutersinstitute.politics.ox.ac.uk/digital-news-report/2022/dnr-executive-summary> (accessed 25 November 2022)

10 Dmitry Shishkin, "Five Lessons I Learned While Digitally Changing BBC World Service", LinkedIn, 3 July 2017 <https://www.linkedin.com/pulse/five-lessons-i-learned-while-digitally-changing-bbc-world-shishkin/>; Jacqueline Woudstra, "5 Questions About the User Needs, With Dmitry Shishkin", *Smartocto*, 28 October 2020 <https://smartocto.com/blog/5-questions-about-user-needs/> (both accessed 14 December 2022)

11 Sylvia Chan-Olmsted and Rang Wang, "Understanding Podcast Users: Consumption Motives and Behaviors", *New Media & Society*, 24:3 (2022), 684–704 <https://doi.org/10.1177/1461444820963776>; Team Whistle, *Ear to the Ground Report*, 2020 <https://teamwhistle.com/insights/2020/11/ear-to-the-ground> (accessed 14 December 2022)

12 Rosalind Coward, *Speaking Personally: The Rise of Subjective and Confessional Journalism* (Basingstoke: Palgrave Macmillan, 2013)

13 Steven Pinker, *The Sense of Style: The Thinking Person's Guide to Writing in the 21st Century* (London: Penguin, 2014)

14 Esther Tolkoff, "Audiobooks: Actors Bring Books to Life", *Backstage*, 4 November 2019 <https://www.backstage.com/magazine/article/audiobooks-actors-bring-books-life-33045/> (accessed 6 June 2023); Saskia Elizabeth Ziolkowski, *Kafka's Italian Progeny* (Toronto: University of Toronto Press, 2020); Donald Murray, "Inside the Writing Process with Don Murray", *Poynter*, 15 November 2004 <https://www.poynter.org/reporting-editing/2004/inside-the-writing-process-with-don-murray/> (accessed 6 June 2023)

15 The clickthrough rate (CTR) is a measure of the number of people who click on a link expressed as a percentage of the number of people to whom the link was sent or shown.

16 Sarah Ebner and Michael Hoole, "How the Financial Times Got More than 78,000 Replies to a Survey", *Inbox Collective*, 19 October 2022 <https://inboxcollective.com/financial-times-newsletter-reader-survey/> (accessed 13 December 2022)

17 Nicole Fenton and Kate Kiefer Lee, *Nicely Said*

18 Rebecca Solnit, *Whose Story is This? Old Conflicts, New Chapters* (London: Granta, 2019)

19 Ronan Krznaric, *Empathy: A Handbook for Revolution* (London: Ebury, 2014)

20 I've used the Empathy Map Canvas designed by Dave Gray of XPLANE with many different student and client groups. You can find the canvas and instructions for how to use it here: <https://medium.com/the-xplane-collection/updated-empathy-map-canvas-46df22df3c8a> (accessed 2 August 2023)

21 Seth Godin, *This is Marketing* (London: Penguin Business, 2019)

2 How we respond to stories

The Story Funnel

This chapter explores what happens when someone reads or listens to a story. Drawing inspiration from individuals who build relationships through online storytelling, it considers how stories attract, involve and influence readers and listeners. The chapter covers:

- Defining story
- How stories gain attention
- How we make sense of the stories we're told
- Identifying with a story and imagining what's happening
- Getting lost in story
- Influencing through story

When was the last time someone told you a story? As a child? During a work presentation? On a date? If the storyteller chose their tale well, I'll wager that you willingly gave them your attention. By telling a story they forged a connection with you, enhancing the odds that you'd remember them and the story they shared.

If winning and maintaining attention is the online writer's greatest challenge, stories offer the perfect solution. Stories hijack our minds before cocooning us away from distraction. When we emerge at the end, like any traveller returning home after an intense journey, we're changed in some way. Stories may make us feel happy or sad, comfortable or unsettled, excited or concerned – whatever, they make us feel *something*.

Though the common image of a storyteller is of a person *telling* a story to a passive listener, listeners and readers play far more active roles than this. Stories aren't simply told. They're *made* by the people who read or listen to them. When you hear or read a well-told story, you become invested in it. You relate to the people within the story and their predicaments, you imagine yourself in their world, and you care about what happens next. While the storyteller decides which information to share, it is you – the reader or listener – who

DOI: 10.4324/9781003363347-3

constructs the story you take away, by processing what you hear in light of your own personal experiences.

Stories entertain, inform, immerse, inspire, and influence. They embed themselves in our brains and change how we think. They even compel us to take action that comes at some personal cost. The impact of sharing a story can be so powerful that literary scholar Jonathan Gottschall describes storytelling as, "witchery".[1]

If you understand how people respond to stories, you'll be well-equipped to deploy these mind-bending tools. You'll appreciate why brands, politicians, and individuals use story, and you'll begin to understand how impactful stories are constructed (an issue we'll return to in Chapter 5). In this chapter, we explore what happens when a reader or listener encounters a story – from an initial state of mental and physical alertness to adopting a new mindset. But first, let's consider what we mean when we say the word "story".

Defining story

When I gained my first serious narrative nonfiction writing contract, I knew very little about what stories were and why they mattered. I consulted articles and books, only to keep reading the same mantras: stories are everywhere ... our brains are hard-wired for story ... stories have power ... stories help us make sense of the world ... stories are memorable and marketable ... Sadly, none of these clichés helped me make much practical sense of what a story actually *is* or what stories *do*, particularly in a nonfiction setting.

Today, after much more research and writing, I finally understand that the essence of any story is remarkably simple. All stories introduce us to someone facing some kind of challenge and then show us what happens next. One of my favourite descriptions of story comes from Lisa Cron. In her book *Story Genius*, Cron explains that the spark of any story comes from how the main person within it makes sense of what's happening: "how she struggles with, evaluates, and weighs what matters most *to her*, and then makes hard decisions, moving the action forward".[2] Well-crafted prose plays a role, but prose only becomes a *story* if you have a person facing a challenge. Readers and listeners are drawn into stories because they're eager to know how that person overcomes that challenge.

Story vs narrative

In some academic fields, researchers distinguish between two different story-related terms.

1 The information and events recounted by the storyteller (which they call the "story"). and
2 The version of events produced and interpreted by the reader or listener (which they call a "narrative").

This distinction means that people *tell stories*, while readers and listeners *make narratives*. In other contexts, however, the term narrative is used interchangeably with story. Personally, I tend to use "story" for both aspects of storytelling, since I find it less formal. That's the convention I've followed in this book.

The Story Funnel

When someone reads or listens to a story, they're taken on an emotional journey. Think about how *you* experience stories. You may be ambivalent at the start, but end up on the edge of your seat. You may grow to care so much about someone in the story that you simply have to get to the end, even if your time and attention is needed elsewhere. You may become so affected by what happened that you can't wait to tell someone else about it. These are all emotional responses.

Though the essence of story is simple, the processes that prompt our responses to story are complex and intertwined. One way to simplify what's going on is to think about the experience of reading or listening to a story like passing through a funnel, which sucks readers in and pulls them deeper and deeper into the world of the story (see Figure 2.1).

Figure 2.1 The Story Funnel: from attracting, involving, and transporting to transforming and acting

In this model, people who stick with a story become more caught up in it as they journey through it. It's similar in concept to the idea of the marketing funnel, which illustrates how marketing activities convert a large pool of disinterested strangers into smaller and smaller numbers of purchasers and followers. The key stages in the traditional marketing funnel are attention, interest, desire, and action. The stages of the Story Funnel are listed below.

1 **Attract.** Potential readers or listeners notice something about a story that sparks their interest. They pay attention.
2 **Involve.** Readers and listeners imagine and interpret what's going on. They relate to a person in the story and the challenge they face. They become involved in their fate.
3 **Transport.** Readers and listeners get carried away. Real-world distractions and influences hold little sway over them.
4 **Transform.** Readers and listeners emerge changed. They think or feel differently.
5 **Act.** Readers and listeners do something. They respond to their new understanding of the world by taking action.

Though some of these stages merge and overlap, representing them as a sequence makes sense, since each stage requires readers and listeners to experience some aspect of the stage before it.

The Story Funnel framework helps us think about what stories do. More importantly, it shows us what we as writers must focus on to help readers and listeners become involved and transported. By separating out the individual processes involved in reading or listening to a story, the Funnel highlights where readers or listeners may be lost; for instance, if we fail to grab their attention, if they aren't able to identify with the challenge the person in the story faces, or if it's too difficult to visualise what's going on. We'll consider the key factors that influence whether readers and listeners make it through each of the Funnel stages below.

Attract

At the start of the Story Funnel, stories gain our attention. As our brains switch onto high alert, we want to know more. We're sucked into the action.

Humans are social creatures. Because we live our lives alongside other people, we have an innate desire to monitor what others think and do. This helps us to judge whether a person or situation might be safe or dangerous, useful or useless. Our natural curiosity is therefore piqued when we notice anything new or different. Like a leopard alert to a shape on the horizon, our brains switch into attentive mode.

On high alert, our hearts pump faster and we breathe rapidly. As blood rushes to our brains, we process information at speed. We actively look for a story because we know it will help us understand what's going on. This story-alert phase is akin to living in a simple video game, like Super Mario Bros., in which a character single-mindedly dashes across a two-dimensional world where everything in their path is either an obstacle to be overcome or something that can help them. In Mario's case, we see everything he does (leaping over obstacles, jumping on top of enemies, and stocking up on coins and power-ups) in the context of his overall goal (saving the princess).

Stories tap into our innate social needs, our natural brain processes, and our tendency to see everything through a narrow, Super-Mario-type lens. They feed us just enough information to spark this alert state before creating an information gap that makes us want more. If we spot someone in a high-stakes situation – or a situation that resonates with our own experience – we can't help but stick around. Of course, some potential readers or listeners will pay attention for a moment, before concluding there's nothing to worry about. Their brains silence the alert and they look away, contributing to the reader-loss statistics we met in Chapter 1. When we're interested, though, we're soon swept into someone else's world.

Involve

During the involve stage of the Story Funnel, we create our own interpretation about what's going on based on the information we receive. We visualise the world of the story and become emotionally involved in the plight of people within it.

We become involved in stories through two interconnected mechanisms.

1 **Storymaking.** We build our own story from the information we read or hear.
2 **Identification and imagination.** We relate to the person in the story and the trouble they're in, picturing the events they experience.

Let's explore each of these mechanisms now.

Storymaking

Stories invite us to become co-creators. We take the information and events we receive and build our own stories from them.

Have you ever sat in a café and conjured up a story about two people at another table? Or explained a friend's out-of-character behaviour by imagining a story about what's going on behind closed doors? If so, you're not alone. It's human nature to create stories. Listeners and readers also create stories – using material provided by the storyteller.

We create stories to help us understand whatever catches our attention. If we didn't have the ability to make stories, says writer Alex Tizon, "the stuff that happens would float around in some glob and none of it would mean anything".[3] To avoid our brains filling with glob, we automatically integrate new information with our existing knowledge. This helps us develop a plausible story about what we see, read, or hear.

People construct stories out of anything, and I mean *anything*. Experiments with animations of geometric shapes show that people instinctively make meaning from meaningless movements. We do this by creating stories – stories influenced by each of our past life experiences.

In practice: making stories from shapes

In 1944 two psychologists showed 34 students a two-and-a-half-minute-long black-and-white film and asked them to write down what happened. **If you're not a fan of spoilers, you might like to watch the film yourself before reading on. Search for 'Heider and Simmel film' on YouTube to find it.**

The film showed a large triangle, small triangle, and small circle moving inside and outside a rectangular box, as illustrated by the stills in Figure 2.2. All but one of the students interpreted the movements of the shapes as actions of animate beings. Most identified them as people; two described them as birds. More than half described what they saw as a coherent story; for instance, telling a tale of two men (the triangles) fighting over a girl (the circle).

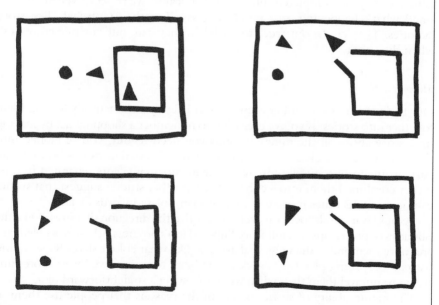

Figure 2.2 Stills from the Heider and Simmel triangles and circle film

In a second stage of the experiment, students were asked to describe what kind of people the shapes were and why they were fighting. Most considered the large triangle to be a mean, aggressive bully, while the small triangle was brave, defiant, and heroic. In contrast, the circle was thought to be shy and helpless. The most common explanation for the fight was that the bully didn't want the hero and the girl to be together. It's a story you'd only concoct if you'd seen or read similar stories in the past, or if you had personal experience of a similar tragic love story.

This experiment has been repeated and adapted many times since. In a version featuring coloured circles, students who reported being unpopular as teens described the shapes as "mad", "crazed", "angry", "blinded by jealousy", and "in a violent narcissistic rage". Those who described themselves as popular at school created a different version of the story. They saw the same actions as benign, even playful.[4]

The geometric shapes studies show that we can't stop ourselves from coming up with a story even when there is none. "Under almost any circumstances", writes psycholinguist Richard Gerrig, "people find it difficult not to create a causal structure to explain some outcome".[5] Our desire to find stories everywhere is both a blessing and a curse. On the one hand, stories helps us to understand the complex world in which we live. On the other, the stories we generate may be completely unfounded. Because we're so driven to understand what's happening, our minds act, says Jonathan Gotschall, like story factories. They churn out true stories when they can, but "manufacture lies" when they can't.[6]

Memory making

Our brains help us remember events in our lives by automatically linking them together into stories. If you've ever tried to remember a shopping list by making up a story about all the different items you need to buy, you've tapped into this trait. It's a sensible strategy, since evidence shows that stories boost recall: participants in one study improved their memory of events separated in time if they combined them into a coherent story; other studies suggest that stories can be up to 12 times more memorable than isolated words or facts.[7]

Because our minds focus on events that drive the direction of a story – like the obstacles or power-ups that influence Super Mario's progress – these story elements are more memorable than less vital aspects (like what colour shoes Super Mario wears).[8] Surprising plot twists stick in the brain too, since we invest more time trying to unravel them than when we're following a straightforward plot.

The memorability of stories is one of the reasons that people use them so much. Want someone to remember your brand name over a competitor? Tell a story. Want your kids to learn to share? Tell them a story. Want the public to wash their hands during a pandemic? Tell a story ... However, we'll only stick with a story if we identify with the person and the trouble they're in.

Identification and imagination

Stories draw us in by showing us the world from someone else's perspective. We identify with that person, imagining the events they experience.

When we identify with someone in a story we feel empathy for them. We adopt their perspective and see the events in the story as they do. When they face a challenge, we feel for them – literally. We experience similar emotions and want them to achieve their goals. If we feel strongly about their fate, we spend time imagining how they might overcome their challenges.[9]

The degree to which we identify with a person in a story is affected by a number of factors.

1 **Similarity.** We're more likely to identify with people like us. That similarity might come from demographic factors, personality traits, or religious or political beliefs. Or we might identify with someone facing a challenge we ourselves face.
2 **Likeability.** We identify more strongly with "good" people, individuals who uphold the norms and values by which we live our own lives. This isn't straightforward though, since we also identify with antiheroes.
3 **Point of view.** We're highly likely to identify with the person from whose perspective the story is written, even if they're dissimilar to us or not particularly likeable.
4 **Inside information.** We're highly likely to identify with a person whose thoughts and emotions are shared in a story, even if they think differently to us.
5 **Realism.** We'll only identify with someone if we believe their experience and emotions to be real.[10]

Because we naturally identify with individuals in a story, if a person or organisation puts themselves in a story, they become more relatable to their audience. As copywriter Christoph Pachucki puts it, organisations tell stories because it helps their brands appear "real, relevant and personal".[11] When brands tell stories, customers start to see them not as huge corporate entities, but as individuals, even friends.

Identifying with struggle

Though we identify with all sorts of people, depending on our own personalities and morals, there's one sort of protagonist people identify with more than most: someone who struggles while attempting to pull-off an unlikely triumph. They might be up against a more advantaged opponent or stuck in seemingly intractable trouble. Either way, we identify because we have struggles too. We want people in stories to succeed because *we* want to succeed;

if the story character overcomes their circumstances, it gives us hope that we might do the same.[12] Writers who share their own vulnerabilities and struggles through story therefore connect with a wide range of people; as brand strategist Ash Rathod's very first post on LinkedIn demonstrates.

In practice: connecting through LinkedIn stories (Ash Rathod)

When brand strategist Ash Rathod first joined LinkedIn, he felt the platform wasn't for him. Viewing it as a website for job-hunters, Rathod didn't feel it was somewhere he could be himself. He didn't give it much thought and ended up writing his first LinkedIn post as a sort of self-therapy.

In the post, Rathod talked about the impact that vitiligo (a skin condition in which patches of skin lose their natural pigment) had on his mental health and how it affected his business. Almost instantly, he regretted sharing such a personal post with his 1,000 or so connections.

Here's the post in full:

"The colour of my skin started to change two years ago …

I began to hide. No camera on video calls and no face to face networking anymore. (And this had a massive impact on my business because I was unable to fully be myself).

As a usually quiet but confident person, the sudden onset of my Vitiligo exacerbated my mental health which was already on an emotional edge due to a huge personal change in my life.

I managed to get through this because I had a family around me who loved me unconditionally.

The other massive pivotal change I remember was one of my clients gave me the space to talk (via email) about these recent changes and sent a really nice message which I'll remember for a long time. It was probably a small thing for her. But a HUGE thing for me.

The reason I post this today is for two reasons.

1 It doesn't take much to be nice to someone else, and give them the words of encouragement they probably need. You don't know how much it will help their wellbeing.
2 It's emotionally draining trying to keep up with what you think others think of you. Be yourself and be kind to yourself. You're good enough. And others know this too.

Once you embrace this, I promise you will be the best version of yourself."

It's an engaging and inspirational post, told in just 231 words. Despite Rathod's fears about sharing his story, the post rapidly racked up 85,000 views and thousands of reactions and comments. People contacted Rathod because they felt inspired, both by what he had been through and by the vulnerability he showed in sharing his personal experience.

Adopting a storytelling strategy

Rathod's next few posts flopped. He finally realised that the reason his first post did so well was because he had told a story. Most people who reacted had little interest in the specific issue that Rathod discussed (an auto-immune disease). Nor did they have much reason to be interested in Rathod himself, since most didn't know him. What people *were* interested in was Rathod's story about overcoming adversity – an experience they could identify with.

Armed with this insight, Rathod applied the principles of storytelling to all his posts. Within in a year he had gained over 20,000 new followers. More importantly, these new connections led to new business opportunities and a new-found confidence.

The experience transformed the way Rathod thought about LinkedIn. It was no longer an impersonal marketplace for jobs but, as Rathod says, "a place where other human beings are … people just like me". Today, Rathod views LinkedIn as a platform where he can attract a like-minded audience simply by telling stories and being himself.

Rathod generously shared everything he's learned about storytelling on LinkedIn in a book called *The Story Link*. It's packed full of advice, including these three pearls of wisdom about connecting with readers.

1 **Pick up on what makes your reader tick.** Go deep on their pain points and engage with them as much as you can (a principle we explored in Chapter 1).
2 **Make every post relevant to your reader.** Think about why you're writing and whether it will matter to your audience.
3 **Incorporate emotion.** If you can get someone feeling, you'll automatically trigger an action.[13]

When we read a story like Rathod's we create a mental image of what happened to him, which makes us feel like we're in the story with him. Readers or listeners will fall out of the Funnel during this stage if they can't make sense of what they're told, if they don't find the main character relatable, or if it's too difficult to picture the scene. If they stick around, though, they enter the world of the story. They become, as psychologists say, "transported".

Transport

During the transport stage of the Story Funnel, we become so carried away that we leave the real world behind. We enter the story world and participate in it.

Stories have the magical ability to transport us to another time and place. As we focus on the story, we escape from the stress and uncertainty of the real world. Multitasking becomes more difficult and we take longer to respond to external demands. We're so wrapped up in the story that we lose track of time.

In some quarters, this experience might be described as "immersion". I've opted to use the term "transported" for two reasons: 1) transportation is the label that psychologists use to denote the specific state of becoming immersed in a story; and 2) being transported captures the idea of not simply entering another world, but of being *taken* there, something that might happen unknowingly or against your will.

In the age of the metaverse you could be forgiven for thinking that immersive experiences belong solely to formats like virtual reality (VR). Increasingly, text or audio storytelling is seen as deficient because it lacks the immediacy and verisimilitude of VR. Yet there's no need to don a VR headset to become transported. While VR users step into pre-built three-dimensional worlds, readers and listeners become immersed in story worlds of their own making.

How readers influence transportation

The extent to which someone is vulnerable to transportation is influenced by:

- The extent to which they pay attention to the story.[14]
- How familiar they are with the topic of the story. For instance, if you know someone similar to a person in a story, who faces similar challenges, you'll experience deeper levels of transportation. This familiarity even changes with the seasons: if you read a story about winter during winter, you're more likely to be transported than if you read it in the spring.[15]
- Whether they are the same emotional state as the emotional tone of the story, which explains why we seek out "weepie" movies when we feel sad.[16]

How writers achieve transportation

Psycholinguist Richard Gerrig suggests that readers can be dispatched on a story journey with little more than an invitation to "abandon the here and now".[17] The depth of transportation depends on a number of story attributes.

- How identifiable the people in the story (and the situations they find themselves in) feel.

- How easy it is to visualise what's happening.
- How realistic the story feels.
- How suspenseful the plot is.[18]

Participating in stories

Once you've accepted the alternate reality of a story world, you participate in it. You desire certain things to happen, you problem solve, and you provide advice about what to do. You even invent new outcomes that you want to see – as avid fan-fiction writers do. This explains why we find ourselves shouting, "don't go into the cellar" while watching a horror film, why we urge a character in peril to look behind them, or why we grow frustrated when a detective in a true-crime drama overlooks a crucial clue.

Participation and transportation act as a virtuous circle: as you participate in a story, you're more likely to feel transported; as you become transported, you're more likely to participate.[19]

Readers or listeners will fall out of the Story Funnel at this stage if there's little suspense or the story lacks authenticity. Those who stay invested are now so detached from the real world that their ability to critically question plummets. They leave their usual beliefs behind and become vulnerable to influence from within the story.

Transform

At the transform stage of the Story Funnel we change. We emerge from the story thinking and feeling differently.

When we travel in real life we do two things: 1) we leave our homes and our day to day lives behind; and 2) we embrace new ways of living. On our return we may say we've expanded our minds or "found" ourselves. Stories have a similar effect. They help us to absorb new information, open our minds to alternative ways of thinking, and provide new perspectives on the world and ourselves. We feel new emotions too, thanks to story-driven hormonal changes.

Emotional and physical change

When you become involved with a story, the hormone oxytocin is released in your brain. Oxytocin is sometimes described as the "love hormone", since it's released when we fall in love. Our oxytocin levels rise when we exercise, when we listen to music, or when we listen to story. High oxytocin levels also boost our empathy for people within the story.

When we're transported by a story, we aren't just mentally distracted from the problems, stresses, and anxieties of real life, our anxiety levels are chemically reduced. Hormonal changes even relieve physical pain, as a study with children in an intensive care unit (ICU) shows.

In practice: pain-relieving stories

Knowing that stories may transport readers and listeners to other places, Brazilian neuroscientist Guilherme Brockington and colleagues set out to test whether storytelling might mitigate the trauma and suffering experienced by children in an ICU.

Brockington and colleagues randomly assigned 81 hospitalised children into two groups. In one group, children chose a story, which was read to them by an experienced storyteller. In the other, children played a riddle game with the same storyteller. Both activities took a similar amount of time. Both felt similarly interactive.

All the children provided saliva samples before and after the story or riddle activity, and each completed a post-activity quiz. The samples showed that, following the activity, children in the story group had double the level of oxytocin than children in the other group, and far lower levels of the stress hormone cortisol. This may help them in a hospital setting because of one or both of these factors.

- Oxytocin reduces psychosocial stress, lessens anxiety and boosts trust. Increased levels may therefore lessen the stress of a hospital stay.
- Cortisol, which is released when we feel under threat, stops our bodies spending energy on systems that aren't required during a run-for-your-life situation, such as digestion and the immune response. Decreased levels may therefore improve your chances of fighting off infection.

Changing minds and alleviating pain

The follow-up quiz showed that this combination of increased oxytocin and reduced cortisol eliminated some of the negative emotions associated with hospitalisation. When shown images of nurses and doctors after the activity, children in the story group described these people in positive terms, using phrases like, "someone who takes care of me" or "a person who helps us get well". In the riddle group, children used descriptions like, "a crabby lady who gives me nasty-tasting medicine" or "a cruel person who pokes me with a needle". What's more, children in the story group reported reduced pain, "at a rate twice as large as those in the riddle group".

While this study didn't measure how long the feel-good response lasted, it's possible that the more we release oxytocin, the more likely we are to release it in the future. If so, the more we read or listen to stories, the more we'll not only escape from our troubles, we'll alleviate them.[20]

Opinion change

The children's ICU research shows that stories have the power to change people's opinions – in that experiment, children's views about doctors and nurses changed after listening to a story. Effects like this are seen again and again in a wide range of contexts. For instance, if you read a story about a holiday destination, you're more likely to view it favourably than if you read the same information presented as a list.[21] If you watch a video story about the human papillomavirus (HPV) on social media, you'll think anew about talking to a healthcare professional about the HPV vaccine.[22] If you support people's right to protest, you'll temper your views after reading a story in which two friends wreck their relationship because they argue about the issue.[23]

We change our minds because, when we're present in a story world, we expend little effort to disbelieve information within the story. Detached from the real world, our beliefs, attitudes, and intentions align with those in the story (even when these beliefs conflict with how we usually think). The deeper we're transported, the greater the effect will be. And, when you've changed you mind about something, you may take action in light of this new knowledge.

Act

Readers and listeners who stick with stories until the act stage of the Story Funnel *do* something in light of their experience. They might like or share a social media post, change their behaviour, or donate or spend money.

If you become transported into a story, you're more likely to take action afterwards. In one experiment, participants listened to a nonfiction podcast in which writer Diane Weipert observes a young couple who live in the apartment opposite her. Over time, Weipert realises that one of the pair has cancer; she then watches his decline and eventual death. After listening, participants completed a questionnaire about their listening experience, which included a question about their willingness to donate money towards cancer research. Those who felt transported into the story had greater willingness to donate than other participants.[24]

Stories – especially those that enable readers or listeners to form rich mental images – are repeatedly seen to be more persuasive than descriptive information and statistics. In another study, college students were split into two groups. The first group learned about Rokia, a seven-year-old girl from Mali who was, "desperately poor" and threatened by "severe hunger, or even starvation". They were then asked how much money they would like to donate to help Rokia. The second group received statistical information about hunger and poverty issues across sub-Saharan Africa, before being asked how much they would like to donate towards reducing hunger in the region. On average, students who learned about Rokia were willing to donate 30 per cent more than students who received statistical information.[25]

Similar results have been seen when comparing the impact of a story about climate change versus statistical descriptions of the issue. Participants who read a climate change story were twice as likely to subscribe to the newsletter of environmental charity Greenpeace and almost twice as likely to recycle the papers they had used during the experiment. Even six weeks later, they were far more likely to respond to an unpaid follow-up survey.[26] Research like this illustrates why stories are so popular with marketeers, who use them for everything from influencing us to buy products to persuading us to invest in new businesses.

In practice: *Good Night Stories for Rebel Girls* origin story

Stories are particularly prevalent on crowdfunding sites like Kickstarter. Successful crowdfunding campaigns usually include an origin story that explains when and how the entrepreneur came up with their business idea. For example, the Kickstarter campaign page for *Good Night Stories for Rebel Girls* (Elena Favilli and Francesca Cavallo's children's book featuring 100 stories about extraordinary women) includes this brief story:

> **"Why a Book for Girls?**
>
> Because we are girls. Our entrepreneurial journey made us understand how important it is for girls to grow up surrounded by female role models. It helps them to be more confident and set bigger goals. We realized that 95% of the books and TV shows we grew up with, lacked girls in prominent positions. We did some research and discovered that this didn't change much over the past 20 years, so we decided to do something about it."

We're then told:

> "We need your help to print the first 1,000 copies, get an ISBN, hire an editor, pay the artists."

The format of this story echoes many others you'll find on Kickstarter and other crowdfunding platforms. Entrepreneurial origin stories tend to emphasise the value of the initial idea, the context in which the idea emerged, and the impact it will have if brought to fruition. They often follow this sort of pattern:

- X years ago I came across a problem.
- I knew it could be done better.

- I spent time developing and testing the idea.
- I created a solution.
- Join me to make the solution happen.

Though the *Goodnight Stories for Rebel Girls* paragraph above doesn't talk about the solution in detail, the entire Kickstarter project page includes sample illustrations and mocked-up images of pages from the book, which demonstrate what the solution will look like.

Why origin stories work

Origin stories in this form influence how readers feel about a number of issues.

- **Authenticity.** Because the entrepreneur has experienced the problem themselves, we feel as if they know what they're talking about.
- **Benevolence.** Because the entrepreneur was willing to do something about the problem, we feel they must be generous and deserving of our support.
- **Intelligence.** Because the entrepreneur overcame a problem, we feel the entrepreneur must be smart and creative, and their business will be successful.
- **Realism.** Because we're told what the next steps are, we feel confident that the idea is feasible.

That's four new opinions which might be swayed in just 100 words.

Stories without statistics work in a crowdfunding context because the entrepreneurs aren't pitching to a bank or venture capitalist (who might want detailed financial information as much as stories) – they're pitching to ordinary people. If potential crowdfunders hear directly from the entrepreneurs, and become involved in *a story*, they may become involved in *the project* too. In a study comparing successful Kickstarter projects with those that fail to secure funding, researchers found that failed campaigns either lacked a clear story pattern or omitted some of the elements we usually expect within a story. In Favilli and Cavallo's case, their project gained over 13,000 backers, who pledged more than $675,000. Not bad when their initial goal was just $40,000.[27]

Our vast understanding of how people respond to stories is growing all the time. As researchers conduct more studies, they create myriad ways to think and talk about how stories affect us. But, fundamentally, people become involved in stories because they spot another person in trouble. If you can find the trouble and organise the events that follow in a suspenseful way, you'll create attention-grabbing stories that involve and influence readers and listeners. In the next chapter we'll meet a set of ingredients that any writer can use to create any story.

Summary

- Stories introduce readers and listeners to someone facing a challenge and then show what happens next.
- Readers and listeners construct stories by combining the information they receive with their existing knowledge.
- People pay attention to a story when they spot something novel or interesting.
- Readers and listeners identify with similar people or people facing similar challenges. They visualise what happens to them, think their thoughts, and feel their emotions.
- When lost in story, readers and listeners participate in the story world. They switch off from reality and become vulnerable to influence.
- Stories may change people's minds, influence their emotions, and drive them to take costly action.
- The more a reader or listener feels transported into a story, the more likely they are to think, feel or act differently.

Practical lessons for online writers

- **Keep your readers and listeners in mind.** Consider what knowledge, attitudes, and values they bring to the story. How might they interpret the details you share? What version of the story might they construct?
- **Give your readers and listeners space.** Allow them to co-create the story, by providing the raw materials they can then combine with their own experiences.
- **Provide sufficient information and detail.** Enable readers and listeners to visualise the scene, understand what is happening, and participate in the action.
- **Choose wisely.** The choices you make about the people in your story, the details you share, and the order in which you reveal information all impact on the likelihood of someone becoming lost in your story.
- **Use stories for good.** Choose to exploit the witchery of stories to build beneficial connections and drive positive change.

Recommended reading

Richard J Gerrig, *Experiencing Narrative Worlds: On the Psychological Activities of Reading* (New Haven, CT: Yale University Press, 1993) – classic text that explores what happens in our brains when we read.

Jonathan Gottschall, *The Storytelling Paradox* (New York: Basic Books, 2021) – insightful perspective on how stories are used, for bad as well as good.

Will Storr, *The Science of Storytelling* (London: William Collins, 2019) – easy-to-read overview of many aspects of story science.

Notes and references

1 Jonathan Gottschall, *The Storytelling Animal: How Stories Make Us Human* (New York: Mariner Books, 2012)
2 Lisa Cron, *Story Genius: How to Use Brain Science to Go Beyond Outlining and Write a Riveting Novel* (New York: Ten Speed Press, 2016)
3 Quoted in Jacqui Banaszynski, "Why We Need Stories", *Nieman Reports*, 15 March 2002 <https://niemanreports.org/articles/why-we-need-stories/> (accessed 10 February 2023)
4 Fritz Heider and Marianne Simmel, "An Experimental Study of Apparent Behavior", *The American Journal of Psychology*, 57:2 (April 1944), 243–59 <https://doi.org/10.2307/1416950>; Mitch Prinstein, *Popular: Why Being Liked is the Secret to Greater Success and Happiness* (London: Vermillion, 2017)
5 Richard J Gerrig, *Experiencing Narrative Worlds: On the Psychological Activities of Reading* (New Haven, CT: Yale University Press, 1993)
6 Jonathan Gottschall, *The Storytelling Animal*
7 Brendan I Cohn-Sheehy et al., "Narratives Bridge the Divide Between Distant Events in Episodic Memory", *Memory & Cognition*, 50 (2022), 478–94 <https://doi.org/10.3758/s13421-021-01178-x>; Gordon H Bower and Michal C Clark, "Narrative Stories as Mediators for Serial Learning", *Psychonomic Science*, 14 (1969), 181–2 <https://doi.org/10.3758/BF03332778>; Chip Heath and Dan Heath, *Made to Stick: Why Some Ideas Survive and Others Die* (New York: Random House, 2007)
8 Melanie C Green, "Transportation into Narrative Worlds", in *Entertainment-Education Behind the Scenes: Case Studies for Theory and Practice*, ed. Lauren B Frank and Paul Falzone (Cham, Switzerland: Palgrave Macmillan, 2021) <https://link.springer.com/chapter/10.1007/978-3-030-63614-2_6> (accessed 2 August 2023)
9 Richard J Gerrig, *Experiencing Narrative Worlds*
10 See, for example, Jonathan Cohen, "Audience Identification with Media Characters", in *Psychology of Entertainment*, ed. Jennings Bryant and Peter Vorderer (Mahwah, NJ: Lawrence Erlbaum Associates, 2006), pp. 183–98 and Suzanne Keen, "A Theory of Narrative Empathy", *Narrative*, 14:3 (October 2006) 207–36 https://www.jstor.org/stable/20107388
11 Christoph Pachucki et al., "No Story without a Storyteller: The Impact of the Storyteller as a Narrative Element in Online Destination Marketing", *Journal of Travel Research*, 61:8 (2022), 1703–18. <https://doi.org/10.1177/00472875211046052> (accessed 2 August 2023)
12 For more on "the underdog effect", see JongHan Kim et al., "Rooting for (and then Abandoning) the Underdog", *Journal of Applied Social Psychology*, 38:10 (October 2008), 2550–73 <https://doi.org/10.1111/j.1559-1816.2008.00403.x>
13 Personal conversation with Ash Rathod, 7 December 2022. See also Ash Rathod, *The Story Link: The Definitive Guide to Storytelling on LinkedIn* (New Founder Hacks, 2022)

14 Tom Van Lauer et al., "The Extended Transportation-Imagery Model: A Meta-Analysis of the Antecedents and Consequences of Consumers' Narrative Transportation", *Journal of Consumer Research*, 40:5 (2014), 797–817 <https://dx.doi.org/10.2139/ssrn.2033192>

15 Melanie C Green and Timothy C. Brock, "In the Mind's Eye", in *Narrative Impact: Social and Cognitive Foundations*, ed. Melanie C Green, JJ Strange and Timothy C. Brock (Mahwah, NJ: Lawrence Erlbaum Associates, 2002); Melanie C Green, "Transportation into Narrative Worlds: The Role of Prior Knowledge and Perceived Realism", *Discourse Processes*, 38:2 (2004), 247–66 <https://doi.org/10.1207/s15326950dp3802_5>

16 Melanie C Green and Marc A Sestir, "Emotion and Transportation into Fact and Fiction", *Scientific Study of Literature*, 2:1 (2012), 37–59 <https://doi.org/10.1075/ssol.2.1.03gre>

17 Richard J Gerrig, *Experiencing Narrative Worlds*

18 Tom Van Lauer et al., "The Extended Transportation-Imagery Model"

19 Richard J Gerrig, "Processes and Products of Readers' Journeys to Narrative Worlds", *Discourse Processes* <https://doi.org/10.1080/0163853X.2023.2177457>

20 Guilherme Brockington et al., "Storytelling Increases Oxytocin and Positive Emotions and Decreases Cortisol and Pain in Hospitalized Children", *PNAS*, 118:22 (2021) <https://doi.org/10.1073/pnas.2018409118>

21 Rashmi Adaval and Robert S Wyer, "The Role of Narratives in Consumer Information Processing", *Journal of Consumer Psychology*, 7:3 (1998), 207–45 <https://doi.org/10.1207/s15327663jcp0703_01>

22 Amy E Leader, "The Impact of HPV Vaccine Narratives on Social Media: Testing Narrative Engagement Theory with a Diverse Range Sample of Young Adults", *Preventative Medicine Reports*, 29 (2022) <https://doi.org/10.1016%2Fj.pmedr.2022.101920>

23 Jonathan Cohen et al., "The Tempering Effect of Transportation: Exploring the Effects of Transportation and Identification During Exposure to Controversial Two-Sided Narratives". *Journal of Communication*, (April 2015), 213–422 <https://doi.org/10.1111/jcom.12144>

24 Anthony G Vaccaro, et al., "Functional Brain Connectivity During Narrative Processing Relates to Transportation and Story Influence", *Frontiers in Human Neuroscience*, 15 (2021) <https://doi.org/10.3389/fnhum.2021.665319>

25 Nathan P Hendricks and Krystal Drysdale, "In-Class Experiment Assesses Empathy for International Hunger and Poverty", *NACTA Journal*, (September 2015), 253–8 <https://www.jstor.org/stable/nactajournal.59.3.253> (accessed 10 February 2023)

26 Brandi S Morris et al., "Stories vs Facts: Triggering Emotion and Action-taking on Climate Change", *Climatic Change*, 154 (2019), 19–36 <https://doi.org/10.1007/s10584-019-02425-6>

27 Kickstarter, *Good Night Stories for Rebel Girls: 11 Tales to Dream Big* <https://www.kickstarter.com/projects/timbuktu/good-night-stories-for-rebel-girls-100-tales-to-dr/description> (accessed 18 January 2023) (Thanks to Rebel Girls, Inc., rebelgirls.com). Stephan Manning and Thomas A Bejerano, "Convincing the Crowd: Entrepreneurial Storytelling in Crowdfunding Campaigns", *Strategic Organization*, 15: 2 (2016) <https://doi.org/10.1177/1476127016648500>

3   Six essential story ingredients

This chapter identifies the six key ingredients that go into making any story. Building on what we've learned about how we experience stories, it pinpoints the specific elements that guide a reader or listener through the Story Funnel. The chapter covers:

- The importance of following a story recipe
- Ingredients that grab attention
- Ingredients that fuel the imagination
- Ingredients that transport or immerse readers and listeners in a story
- Story recipes and the role of artificial intelligence

As a child I once wrote a story about a small cuddly toy named Panda W. I remember this partly because of the toy's intriguing name, but mostly because Panda W still sits on my bookshelf; I feel the gaze of his glassy eyes on the back of my head as I type these words. Yet I remember next to nothing about the story itself.

When I recently sought out the shiny red exercise book where I had scrawled Panda W's tale, it was obvious why I had no memory of it. The story centred around a mysterious-sounding central character, but offered little more. The ingredients that make any story involving, impactful, and memorable were all missing.

Of course, I was young and naive when I wrote the Panda W story-that-wasn't-really-a story, but I made the same mistakes as an inexperienced professional writer. Working with students for many years, I've seen plenty miss the mark because they omitted a crucial story component. And the Internet is full of "our story" web pages that would be vastly improved with the addition of one or two overlooked elements. I find this frustrating because, as we saw in Chapter 2, the essence of a story is remarkably simple. I therefore wrote this chapter to rid the world of stories-that-aren't-really-stories. More realistically, I hope that if you

DOI: 10.4324/9781003363347-4

appreciate the key ingredients that make up every story, you'll be able to write absorbing, impactful, and memorable stories, time and time again.

Why following a recipe makes sense

Some people think that following a recipe or rulebook for storytelling is somehow cheating. Others think that they'll end up with a more original result if they skip the guidance and just do what feels right. If you're aiming to while away years in an attic producing an avant-garde work of literary fiction, both these thoughts may be true. If, like me, you're a nonfiction writer working to tight deadlines, then a set of guidelines is a valuable tool. Pulitzer prize-winning journalist Jon Franklin agrees.

In his book *Writing for Story* Franklin describes himself as a "conscious writer", someone who relies on storytelling patterns and principles rather than instinct. Franklin describes stories as "magical", but writing them as "mechanistic".[1] Like Franklin, I'd venture that many writers follow some kind of recipe as they write, even if they do so subconsciously, under the more romantic guise of writerly instinct.

Relying on a set of standard story ingredients has many benefits.

- **Speeding up the process of constructing a story.** If you're a beginner or you lack inspiration while working to a tight deadline, a recipe helps you get started.
- **Keeping you on track.** Recipes help you stay focused on telling a *story*, not playing with words or spewing out a stream of consciousness.
- **Increasing the odds of readers becoming emotionally involved.** The recipe draws, after all, on what we know about how people read and listen, and the factors influencing their level of involvement in a story.
- **Providing a useful checklist when revising and editing.** This may help you deduce what's missing or identify how to save a failing story.
- **Enabling you to take decisions that diverge from the norm.** If you're familiar with the essential ingredients, you can make a conscious decision to try something different. It's the difference between *opting* to spice up a dish and *accidentally* overdoing the chilli.

I deliberately didn't call these key story components "rules" because I don't want them to constrain you. If you familiarise yourself with the ingredients, you'll find it easier to conceive, construct, and sense-check your own stories. But feel free to adapt and extend the ingredients to suit your needs.

In some ways it's a bit like baking. When you're starting out, you'll only get perfect fairy cakes if you follow a recipe. As you become more experienced, you gain more knowledge of what works for you and for the people who eat your food. With this new-found confidence you might then diverge from the recipe that started it all. Perhaps you fold in an additional ingredient, adapt the baking time to the atmospheric conditions in your kitchen, or create a "signature" cake decoration. Overall, you identify what works for you and your audience by building on a body of tried–and-tested knowledge.

The story ingredients that I share in this chapter are an adaptation and extension of Jon Franklin's definition of story. Franklin describes a story as, "a sequence of actions that occur when a sympathetic character encounters a complicating situation that he confronts and solves".[2] This is a useful summary of the essence of any story but when I used this definition with undergraduate students, I realised they needed more guidance. So I created my own set of ingredients, which make it easy to cook up any online nonfiction story.

Story ingredients

The six story ingredients support three different types of reading or listening processes. These align with the first three stages of the Story Funnel, which we introduced in Chapter 2. These focus on attracting, involving, and transporting readers or listeners into a story.

1 **Ingredients that attract**
    These identify who your story is about and the challenge they face, so readers want to know more.
        Ingredient 1: person
        Ingredient 2: challenge
2 **Ingredients that involve**
    These show where and when your story happens and conjure up the world of the story, so readers and listeners may become involved.
        Ingredient 3: setting
        Ingredient 4: detail
3 **Ingredients that transport**
    These set out what happens to the person in your story, what happens next, and what happens in the end. They transport readers and listeners by building and releasing tension.
        Ingredient 5: sequence of events
        Ingredient 6: resolution

We'll now explore each of these ingredients in turn.

Ingredients that attract

Stories introduce readers and listeners to someone facing a challenge and show them what happens next. The two most important ingredients in a story are *the person who is introduced* and *the predicament they face*.

While every ingredient in this chapter is essential, if you lack the first two, readers and listeners may never give your story a second glance. It is the person and their challenge that gain readers' and listeners' attention, especially in short-form, online nonfiction. They put a potential reader or listener on alert before setting the direction of travel and inviting them along for the ride.

Ingredient 1: person

Nonfiction stories gain and maintain our interest because they're about real people – people who take action and steer the direction of the story. In fiction, you'd usually call these people "characters". I use the term "person" to indicate that this is a real human being.

The person in the story lives through whatever unfolds, providing readers and listeners with a unique perspective from the midst of the action. To demonstrate why people are invaluable, let's look at three opening lines from online articles about a hurricane that struck the United States in 2005. As you read each, think about whether they'd encourage you to read on.

> *Opening line 1*
>
> Tropical cyclone Hurricane Katrina hit the south-eastern United States in August 2005.

> *Opening line 2*
>
> Hurricane Katrina was one of the worst natural disasters in our Nation's history and has caused unimaginable devastation and heartbreak throughout the Gulf Coast Region.[3]

> *Opening line 3*
>
> Cierra Chenier was just 9 years old when Hurricane Katrina struck New Orleans and forced her family to evacuate.

Opening line 1 and 2 focus on the hurricane – we meet Katrina and learn that this tropical cyclone struck the US at a specific time and place. Opening line 1 fails to grab my attention because there's little hint about why this might be an important or interesting event. Opening line 2 gives us some idea of the devastation caused by the hurricane. We may well think about the many people who were affected, which might encourage us to read on. Unlike the other sentences, opening line 3, which kicks off a *Smithsonian Magazine* story, focuses on the impact of the hurricane. It's the only line that encourages *me* to read on, because I immediately want to find out what happened to Cierra.[4]

A single person

Though stories sometimes revolve around multiple people, brain research shows that focusing on a single individual like Cierra makes a tangible difference to readers and listeners. If you take magnetic resonance images of people's brains while they listen to short news stories, a part of the brain that we use when we're appreciating how other people think and feel lights up. This area is more strongly activated, for longer time periods, when a story focuses on one person than if it includes several individuals. Our brains therefore pay less attention to stories about multiple people than stories that focus on one main person.[5] This explains why some based-on-a-true-story tales feature composite characters: imagined individuals who combine the personalities and traits of multiple real people, so that readers and listeners have fewer individuals to connect with.

While it is theoretically possible to create an involving story that revolves around several different people – especially, for instance, if each person's experience tells a different part of the overall story – this is rarely effective in the space constraints of short-form writing. Stories with multiple characters are more often seen in long-form formats, like novels or TV series.

Someone we care about

Though we're innately more interested in people than, for example, hurricanes, we identify with some people more than others. This identification might come from likeability or because we share similar values (even if we look or feel different on the surface). Equally, it may come from the predicament the person faces.

If you've heard people talk about "the hero's journey" in relation to storytelling, you may think the person in your story ought to be a conventional, victorious hero. Not so. The most compelling true stories reflect the complex reality of what it means to be human, a reality that encompasses failure as much as success. As Pixar story artist Emma Coats writes in her widely shared 22 rules of storytelling, "you admire a character for trying more than for their successes".[6] We're drawn to misfits and mavericks too, because, at some time or other, we've felt left out or wished we had the guts to break the rules.

Flawed people

Writing about flawed individuals creates opportunities to explore people's inner turmoil. Traditional "character arcs", familiar from long-form fiction, like films, TV shows and books, follow a character as they acknowledge and overcome a personal weakness to get what they want. This approach is less common in the short-form nonfiction seen or heard online, since there's limited space to reveal the depth of a person's character or to chronicle a full transformational arc. Even when space is available, it may be difficult to construct an arc for a real person, unless the writer has privileged access to what was going on inside their head. If you're writing about yourself, this may be an appealing approach. If you're not, only proceed if you're confident you have enough information to reveal someone's inner thoughts.

Ingredient 2: challenge

Readers and listeners are drawn into a story when a person encounters some kind of complication or challenge. As an example, here's the opening sentence of the first episode of true-crime podcast *Serial*, as told by series narrator and journalist Sarah Koenig:

> For the last year, I've spent every working day trying to figure out where a high-school kid was for an hour after school one day in 1999.[7]

At this stage in the *Serial* story we don't know anything about that high-school kid (Adnan Syed, who we later discover is serving time in a maximum-security prison for the murder of his girlfriend, despite claiming innocence). Instead, it is the narrator's challenge that draws us in: Koenig needs to find out where Adnan Syed was at 2.30pm on 13 January 1999. To solve this puzzle, she must identify witnesses, track them down, and extract information from them. As we progress through the episode, we realise there is another aspect to this challenge: when witness statements don't align, who should Koenig believe?

In his book *The Storytelling Animal*, academic and writer Jonathan Gottschall describes the key ingredient of story as "trouble".[8] Sometimes that trouble is simply someone wanting something they don't have – like a job, money, or a romantic interest. Sometimes it's a practical challenge (like trying to find out where a teenager was on a winter afternoon 15 years earlier). Other times it's an emotional or psychological one (like working out which teenager to trust). In the best stories, it's often both, though the psychological element may not be obvious to the reader (or even the writer) in the beginning. I once taught a student who wrote a story about the trials and tribulations of buying his first suit. Only as he developed and redrafted his story did he realise that the engine driving his story was growing up. For this young writer, buying a suit was a snapshot of the far greater challenge he faced at the time: becoming a man.

Conflict by another name

You'll sometimes hear the trouble at the heart of a story described as "conflict" or "tension". I prefer "challenge" because it highlights *the thing* that causes that conflict; you can't just "write conflict" but you can create tension by identifying and introducing a challenge. This tension drives readers and listeners toward the end of the story because humans are natural tension reducers.

This holds true even if we already know how a story ends. In that case, we want to discover *how* the challenge was resolved.

A challenge that matters

The challenge, says John Yorke, usually "throws your protagonist's world out of kilter" causing "an explosion of sorts in the normal steady pace of their lives".[9] At the launch of *Serial*, Koenig makes it clear that finding out where Adnan Syed was that afternoon had consumed her for a year. For the student buying a suit, he stood at a crucial pivot point in life, where everything about him and his place in the world was changing. The challenge has to *matter* to the person in the story, else why should readers or listeners care?

Even seemingly mundane challenges can matter depending on the context of the story. Another student on the same course as the suit-buyer wrote a story about getting ready to go out to a nightclub. It didn't sound that compelling to me – until she explained the challenge she faced as a feminist: she felt pressured to dress in decidedly non-feminist garb when she was preparing for a big night out. The trouble at the heart of this student's story was a head full of frustration about why she should submit to the patriarchy in order to have fun. Getting dressed may not sound like it matters. Getting dressed in heteronormative club gear when you're an ardent feminist does.

External vs internal challenges

Unless they're writing about themselves, online nonfiction writers tend to focus on tangible external challenges (like finding your way, getting a job, or recovering from illness) not internal ones (like dealing with anxiety, overcoming imposter syndrome, or learning to love oneself). That's because they have limited space to tell stories and limited access into other people's minds. By necessity, online nonfiction usually engages readers and listeners through the actions the person in the story takes in order to overcome the challenge. However, if you're writing about yourself, or about someone you're able to interview at length, you may, as we've already seen, have access to privileged information.

Shared challenges

The most powerful story challenges are ones that we all relate to – fundamental human issues like love, pain, and loss. Issues like this transform a story about one individual into a story of shared experiences. The Museum of Broken Relationships, a crowdsourced online museum with physical outposts in Zagreb and Los Angeles, taps into these shared needs and experiences. The Museum, which describes itself as, "a museum about you, about us", collects stories as much as objects. These stories cover the familiar experiences of love and loss. Since most people identify with these themes, visitors to the Museum website empathise with others' stories, whoever they are and wherever they live.

This is the great paradox of effective storytelling: people will be more engaged if you tell a specific story about an individual's unique experience, but people become engaged because that individual story is representative of a common, shared experience. This is why stories of shared challenges have the power to build communities who take collective action, something we'll explore in more depth in Chapter 4.

Ingredients that involve

A setting, along with visual and contextual detail, helps readers and listeners visualise what is happening in a story. Without these elements, people may not become involved, or they may struggle to understand what's going on. With them, readers and listeners see what the person in the story sees, feel what they feel, and interpret what's happening.

Ingredient 3: setting

Stories are specific. They describe discrete moments and events, not general habits or behaviours. Every story needs a specific setting, one which your reader or listener might easily picture. As an example, compare these two opening lines:

> *Opening line 1*
>
> Claire Hastie often found it hard to breathe.

> *Opening line 2*
>
> When Claire Hastie, a single mother to three boys, woke on Mother's Day in March 2020 finding it hard to breathe, she knew something was wrong.[10]

Pause for a moment and ask yourself:

- Which of these openings makes me want to read on?
- Which offered the most information about when and where the story took place?
- Which helped me picture the scene?
- Which helped me imagine myself in that moment?

Opening line 1 is short and to the point, with a hint of mystery. It makes us want to know who Claire is and why she finds it hard to breathe. If we're familiar with how stories work, we might expect this snippet of information to lead somewhere interesting. For instance, perhaps the second sentence would say, "Today, she could barely catch a breath". This opening sentence does, therefore, grab attention and encourage people to read on.

In comparison, though, opening line 2 has greater potential to engage a reader. Taken from a World Health Organization story about living with long Covid (which was shared online and on Instagram), the sentence delivers a sense of time and place, and a feeling of urgency. We assume Claire is in bed, in the morning. Since we all have some experience of waking up, we imagine ourselves in that situation, too. Unlike opening line 1, it conjures up a rich, dynamic image where a real person *does* something: a woman wakes up, gasps for breath, and worries. This sentence therefore does three important jobs: it grabs attention, encourages people to read on, *and* helps readers picture what's happening.

The specific setting of any story reaches beyond the basics of location and time. It might involve mood, colour, sound, smell, and taste. To satisfy your readers' or listeners' obvious questions, the setting should be established early on, often in the first line or paragraph. You can then maintain a sense of place by incorporating additional, small details throughout the story. If the time or location change at any point, you'll need to signal this clearly.

Ingredient 4: detail

In tandem with events and actions that push a story forward, stories need visual information and contextual detail. While these ingredients are some-times termed "descriptive" and "explanatory" details I use the terms visual and contextual here – for reasons that should become apparent. [11]

Visual detail

Visual details help us to *visualise* what is happening. For example, look at these two sentences and consider their impact on you as a reader:

> Details 1
>
> When she stood up, a pile of random things fell from her lap.

> Details 2
>
> When she stood up, a fuss of receipts, tissues, clip-on earrings and biscuit crumbs fell from her lap. [12]

Both sentences serve the same explanatory purpose in this story, since each informs us that a woman collects unexpected items in her lap. However, the second version – taken from an online article that Georgie Evans wrote about visiting her grandmother – helps readers create a mental image of the scene.

Visual details like this convince us of a story's lifelikeness. "Concrete details, realistic details, details of real life", says author Ted Cheney, deliver the emotional context of the story. [13] The mental images conjured up by specific visual details therefore play a vital role in keeping readers and listeners in a story.

Contextual detail

Context details help us understand the wider *context* of the story events, so we're able to interpret what's happening. In the same article excerpted above, Evans later writes of her grandmother:

> She collected and stashed things, and it was almost impossible to convince her to throw anything away. She lived in defence of her belongings, trying to per-suade us that she needed every single thing she owned.

These details – which come from Evans's wider knowledge of her grand-mother's behaviour – help us understand that Evans's grandmother hoarded things. If they weren't there, our storymaking brains might concoct any num-ber of reasons to explain why this woman had receipts, earrings, and biscuit crumbs in her lap. Or we might be so confused about what's going on that we'd drop out of the story in frustration. Context details like this keep read-ers and listeners engaged, while guiding them to construct the story that the writer intends.

Selecting details

The most impactful details are what writer Lee Gutkind calls "intimate details".[14] This isn't a reference to tawdry information about people's sex lives. For Gutkind, intimate details communicate, "a memorable truth" about the people or situations you describe. They're details that a reader or listener wouldn't otherwise know; scenes you've observed yourself, dialogue you've captured, or unexpected information uncovered in your research. While intimate details may be fascinating, don't overdo them. Every detail you share should serve a purpose in the story.

When choosing what details to include, remember that your audience may already possess some relevant knowledge. If you're able to tap into what's in your reader's or listener's head, you can provide just enough infor-mation for them to fill the gaps themselves. Even better, blend your details into the action, so readers and listeners aren't distracted from the events that drive the story on. We'll explore this "show don't tell" approach more in Chapter 6.

Ingredients that transport

The final story ingredients are a sequence of events and a resolution. They take the person in the story (and the reader or listener) on a journey from the status quo, through a challenging time to a new world. Without these ingredients, readers and listeners won't become involved enough to be transported.

Ingredient 5: sequence of events

Once an audience is engaged by a relatable person and a challenge that matters, stories set out a sequence of events to show how the person resolves the problem. Though this ingredient falls far down our list of six, it's as important as the person and their challenge. If your story lacks a sequence of events it will be confusing or plain dull. With one, you'll build tension through suspense. Readers and listeners will stick around because, as journalist and podcaster Ira Glass says, "whenever there's a sequence of events – this happened, then that happened, then this happened – we inevitably want to know what happened next".[15]

Let's compare two stories to see this in practice:

Story 1

When California-based trainer Leo Babauta found the constant stream of work and personal messages overwhelming, he wanted something to change. Within a month he had declared himself independent from email.

Story 2

California-based trainer Leo Babauta once checked email multiple times a day. He felt as if he was constantly on-call, and he spent an overwhelming amount of time crafting replies, unsubscribing from newsletters, and deleting spam.

Babauta set up automatic filters, moved low-priority emails to a dedicated folder, and even set up a separate email address for key contacts. None of this stopped email from becoming an unenjoyable chore. Babauta decided he needed to phase it out.

He thought about how to communicate and collaborate without sending a single email, and set up alternative communication channels for different people and purposes. His email autoresponder explained how to contact him. In most cases, this advised people to connect via Twitter.

One benefit of using Twitter is brevity – the character limit on tweets forces people to write short messages. Another is that expectations of receiving a reply are far lower than for email. For longer conversations, Babauta used instant messaging and phone or video chat. His friends and family were expected to call.

Babauta announced his independence from email in a blog post, saying, "I'm done". His no-email life is a manifestation of a key professional principle: that no one should be controlled by dreary, ineffective communication systems.

Both these stories include a real person (Leo Babauta), a challenge (dealing with an overwhelming volume of email), and an end point (becoming independent from email). In Story 1, we jump almost instantaneously from the challenge to the end. It happens so fast, we end up thinking the challenge wasn't that challenging in the first place. There's little tension and therefore limited desire to read on. Stories like this make me feel cheated, as if I've been tossed a few tidbits rather than offered a complete meal. This sense of wanting is exploited by some brand storytellers, who share a challenge and an end result (as I've done in story 1), before encouraging readers to visit their website to access the missing part of the story (the part that shows us how the result was achieved).

In Story 2 – which I wrote for an online learning resource about business communication – we're guided through a sequence of events, even if some are implied rather than explicit.[16]

1 Babauta realises email is a drain on his time and energy.
2 He attempts to solve the problem by filtering and prioritising messages.
3 He sets up an alternative email address for key contacts.
4 He's still unhappy.
5 He thinks about how he can communicate without using email.
6 He asks most people to contact him via Twitter, instant messaging, or phone/video chat.
7 He asks friends and family to phone him.
8 He declares himself independent of email.

This version of the story is more useful because we learn something about how Babauta achieved his goal. If the audience is interested in the challenge, it will hold their attention longer. They go on a journey with Babauta; they understand what led him to make a change, they imagine themselves in the same situation, they appreciate what Babauta needed to do to wrestle free from email.

Chronology vs plot

Unlike the stories that we all wrote as children, stories aren't simply a chronological list of everything that happens. Even in nonfiction stories, writers leave information out or reorganise events. This doesn't mean they change the facts, simply that they order the facts in a way that hooks readers and listeners and keeps them interested.

As writer Nora Ephron writes, "I thought stories were simply *what happened*. As a screenwriter I realized that we *create* stories by imposing narrative on the events that happen around us".[17] Just as readers and listeners construct narratives from the snippets of information or actions that writers share, writers themselves construct stories from the facts they gather. Think about the true stories you share all the time. If I asked you to tell me a story about how your last relationship ended or why you're reading this book, what would you say? Do you start by telling me *everything*? Or will you pick out key events and share them in an order that makes sense for the story you want to tell? It's likely you'll compress some aspects or flip back and forth in time, all so you can tell a more involving story.

Playing with time enables writers to construct suspenseful plots from what might, at first, feel like flimsy material. When you stretch out time, every fleeting moment becomes part of the sequence of events. If you compress time, events that happened hours, days, or even years apart come together to form one coherent story.

Whatever events you share, in whatever order, they *must* drive the action forward. If you want readers and listeners to understand how one event caused another, each must follow seamlessly from the one before. And every event must take the story one step closer to the resolution of the challenge.

Ingredient 6: resolution

All stories reach some kind of ending – a moment when the writer stops, even if events continue in real life. At this end point, two things happen.

1 The person in the story takes action to resolve the challenge we met earlier.
2 Any other loose ends are tidied up.

Resolutions may be happy, sad, or, as is the case with most true stories, somewhere in between. They involve the person in the story changing the world around them in some way, changing themselves, or both. Memorable resolutions include a twist, as this example from essayist Jacqueline Dooley shows. It's the end of a story about getting a dog (named Roo), not because Dooley wanted it, but because her daughter insisted.

> Sometimes I'm convinced that this was my daughter's plan all along – to give me something to focus my parental energy on, something else to love that would love me in return. Roo soothes the ache deep within my broken heart by offering up nothing more than companionship and love. And that's how, at the ripe old age of 51, I've suddenly discovered that I am, indeed, a dog person.[18]

The twist comes when we realise that Dooley's daughter, who was dying, may have planned the outcome. Ultimately, we see a change in Dooley: she has become a dog person (despite only ever owning cats before).

For maximum effect, resolutions should centre on the action of the person, not some extraneous event. For instance, if a story features a person tied down on a train track, a resolution in which they're saved because the train breaks down is far less impactful than one in which the person draws on their spirit and ingenuity to wrestle themselves free. Of course, in true stories, you don't have licence to change the ending, but you may be free to choose which stories to tell based on what happens at the end. Working backwards from the resolution can help you work out who plays the biggest role in the story's ending – you might then tell the story from their perspective instead. Alternatively, you may start with a different challenge. In the train track example, perhaps the core challenge isn't being tied to the tracks, but the person's selfish nature, an attribute that changes because of their near-death experience.

Unsatisfactory endings

Readers and listeners find endings satisfying because they release dramatic tension. Think how unsatisfied you feel when you reach the end of a story and still don't know what happened. I experienced this recently, when I was left with a burning question after listening to a news report that went something like this:

> John Brown and his son were driving down the M62 motorway on their way to collect a new kitten when they spotted a car moving unusually slowly in the fast lane. When Brown drew alongside the vehicle he saw the driver slumped over his steering wheel. He pulled into the fast lane and slowed down. The rogue vehicle hit Brown's bumper three times before coming to a standstill. Brown rushed over to administer first aid. Thanks to his efforts, the driver survived.

Can you guess what my unanswered question was? This story is clearly about two men: one who collapsed while driving in the fast lane and one who noticed him. By the end of the story, we have a resolution for each: one is alive and well, one saved someone's life. But the question in my mind was "What happened to the kitten?" Objectively, I know the kitten isn't the main focus of the story. However, because it was introduced at the start, I paid attention to it. When it wasn't mentioned again, I was left with an image of a kitten sitting all alone waiting for its new owners.

This is an example of a principle known as Chekov's Law, named after Russian playwright Anton Chekov, who reportedly said "If in the first act you have hung a pistol on the wall, then in the following one it should be fired."[19] Like me, Chekov would want to know whether the kitten ever met its new owners or not. A brief final sentence was all the report needed to resolve each of the stories it had started. Either that or the kitten should never have been mentioned.

While it's important not to leave anything *out* of the resolution you also shouldn't throw unnecessary material *in*. Just like a conclusion in an essay, a resolution draws all the previously shared strands together. You should have laid down all the groundwork before you get there, so the resolution flows seamlessly from the preceding events and actions.

Multilayered resolutions

In stories where writers have sufficient time and information to be able to explore the inner world of the central person, the resolution may be multilayered. One aspect of the resolution is what happened in terms of the challenge. Another aspect is what happened to the person themselves – did they learn something, did they change their attitude, did they develop a new skill?

Even when online writers don't spend a huge amount of time exploring people's inner worlds, they may still be able to show how an individual changes, especially if that change is simply a shift in knowledge or understanding. For instance, the resolution of the challenge in the first episode of *Serial* is simply that narrator Sarah Koenig has gained some additional knowledge. By the end of the episode, Koenig has spoken with a witness (who didn't give evidence at Adnan Syed's trial) who says she saw Syed in the library at the exact moment when the State claimed he was strangling a young woman. Though we don't know whether Koenig has changed on an emotional level, it's clear that she knows more about what happened on that day now. Plus, she's gained insight into the nature of Syed's court defence.

The human ingredient

Reducing storytelling to a set of common ingredients, as I have done in this chapter, prompts an important question: if stories are made by following recipes, couldn't a computer just follow the recipe for you? With the advent of artificial intelligence (AI) writing programs, the answer is, to some extent, yes.

By scouring tens of thousands of online books, articles, and websites, AI writing programs have learned how other people write. They know which combinations of words are most commonly used and apply this knowledge to generate new content, including stories. If you want, they'll edit your own writing too. When I asked an AI writing partner (who's on call 24 hours a day and who's read far more than any human) to extend the first few sentences of this chapter it responded with this:

> My writing was terrible. It took me several attempts to read my six-year-old efforts, as the words and letters leapt off the page in a green blur that was difficult to focus on.

While this AI-generated text feels plausible, it's also problematic. That "green blur" makes little sense. More worryingly, the program invented my age, which may or may not be true. When I told the system I intended to write the Panda W story anew, it wrote:

> It doesn't matter, because now I'm the one who gets to call the shots. This time Panda W will be a panda detective.

Again, this doesn't quite deliver, since I called the shots in my childhood version too. I do, however, like the idea of Panda W being recast as a detective. This highlights a key benefit of AI writing partners: they might inspire you to take your story in unexpected directions.

Statistical storytelling

Though it's tempting to get carried away by all the possibilities – both positive and negative – of AI writing, it's worth thinking for a moment about how these systems work. Stories created by AI are influenced by whatever content their machine learning models have been trained on. Like a more sophisticated version of auto-complete, when these "large language models" (LLMs) are given a question or prompt they search for patterns in previously published writing and generate text based on a statistical guess of what makes sense. This has three important consequences.

1 Though AI-generated text sounds like it's been written by someone who knows what they're talking about, it hasn't. If the system learns that phrases like, for example, "rising inflation" and "raising interest rates" often appear together, it can write an article that suggests raising interest rates as a suitable strategy to deal with inflation. Yet it has no fundamental understanding of what inflation or interest rates are, or of how interest rates impact inflation.
2 By generating text based on what has been written before, AI writing programs are inherently conservative. Influenced by the majority not the minority, they're unlikely to generate anything truly original.
3 AI writers are fed by online content authored, as Elizabeth Weil has written, by people who "overrepresent white people. They overrepresent men. They overrepresent wealth".[20] AI-generated text may therefore perpetuate the views and biases of these people at the expense of others. A quick experiment shows how this can pan out. When I repeatedly asked ChatGPT to write a story about two people in an office, whom I named Andi and Abdul, nine out of ten versions of the story described Andi as creative, a term never applied to Abdul. Conversely Abdul was almost always described as meticulous, methodical, or analytical. He was sometimes "calm" (which was never said about Andi), while Andi was usually "outgoing", "energetic", or

"enthusiastic" (words never used to describe Abdul). Though a statistically small experiment, these results suggest an inbuilt bias that someone named Andi will be creative and outgoing, while someone named Abdul will be quiet and methodical.

Why we still need writers

Though we can never know what tomorrow will bring, it feels like the world still needs writers – at least for the foreseeable future.[21] Just as spell and grammar checkers fail to identify some errors, while introducing others, AI writing programs are at their most useful when accompanied by human expertise. AI may learn from what has been written before, but humans learn from what's going on in the world around them – including learning from people and events that are yet to be written about. AI programs may generate content far more rapidly than a human writer, but they lack the writer's empathic superpower. Only a human can empathise with the subject of a story. Only a human understands how to connect authentically with readers and listeners.

This connection is key. For writer William Zinsser, the heart of nonfiction writing is, "a personal transaction" between writer and reader or listener.[22] The main product that any writer sells, says Zinsser, isn't the story they produce but they, themselves – it's their enthusiasm, the emotional baggage they bring to the topic, and the part of themselves they leave on the page. The best nonfiction writers convey information by revealing a picture of the world that they – and only they – have observed. So, while Jon Franklin considers the process of writing to be mechanistic, he emphasises that it's "you", the writer, who transforms a set of formulaic ingredients into the magic of story. And it's you who can choose to tell stories that haven't been told before.

As AI storytelling systems improve, and acceptable rules for use become established, they may become as ubiquitous as spellcheckers. If you worry that this makes your job redundant, you devalue yourself. Your ability to understand complex issues, to empathise, and to think beyond what has been written before makes you far more valuable than statistically driven AI systems. Readers and listeners will benefit from the decisions that only you can make about what stories to tell, how best to tell them, and what you're aiming to achieve. In the next chapter we'll consider what drives people to tell stories online and how writers can make a difference in the world.

Summary

- Every story needs six ingredients: a person; a challenge; a setting; detail; a sequence of events; and a resolution.
- Readers and listeners pay less attention to a story that follows multiple people than one centred on a single person.

- Short-form nonfiction tends to spend more time describing someone's actions than sharing their inner thoughts. This is especially true when we're writing about someone other than ourselves.
- The challenge the person in the story faces may be practical or psychological. Either way, it should matter to them – and to the reader or listener too.
- A specific setting, visual details, and contextual information all enable readers and listeners to visualise the story world and interpret what's happening.
- The sequence of events builds tension and suspense. These events may be presented in any order, so long as they take readers or listeners on a coherent journey towards the resolution.
- Resolutions relieve the dramatic tension in a story. Following seamlessly from the preceding events, they show how the person in the story resolved the challenge, while tying up any loose ends. Where space and access to information allow, resolutions may also reveal how the person has changed.
- A writer's knowledge and experience play an important role in choosing and mixing the story ingredients to create a unique and compelling story, which only they could write.
- AI writing programs are able to generate stories by looking for patterns of word use in masses of online content. Unlike human writers, they lack comprehension and empathy. Like the content that fuels them, they may exhibit bias.

Practical lessons for online writers

- **Tell specific stories that echo common, shared experiences.** Readers and listeners identify with real people facing relatable challenges.
- **Gather your ingredients before you start writing.** Choose a relatable person, an appropriate setting, and a challenge that matters. Select a sequence of events that show how the person tackles the challenge, compile visual and contextual details that help us understand what is happening, and identify a tension-releasing resolution.
- **Drive your story forward with action.** Focus on what the person does to overcome the challenge – in their mind and in their actions.
- **Don't be a slave to chronology.** Select and rearrange events to form a plot that involves readers or listeners and builds suspense.
- **Be confident in your perspective.** Stick to the facts, but tell the story only you can tell.
- **Value yourself.** You have empathy, creativity, and a connection with the real world. You understand what's going on in the world and can make a difference by choosing to tell untold stories.

Recommended reading

Jon Franklin, *Writing for Story: Craft Secrets of Dramatic Nonfiction by a Two-Time Pulitzer Prize Winner* (New York: Plume, 1994) – excellent exploration of the nonfiction storyteller's craft, which provided much of the inspiration for this chapter.

John Yorke, *Into the Woods: How Stories Work and Why We Tell Them* (London: Penguin, 2013) – a comprehensive introduction to how stories are constructed.

Notes and references

1 Jon Franklin, *Writing for Story: Craft Secrets of Dramatic Nonfiction by a Two-Time Pulitzer Prize Winner* (New York: Plume, 1994)
2 Ibid.
3 <https://georgewbush-whitehouse.archives.gov/reports/katrina-lessons-learned/chapter1.html> (accessed 2 August 2023)
4 <https://www.smithsonianmag.com/smart-news/black-children-hurricane-katrina-tell-their-stories-180980668/> (accessed 2 August 2023) (Copyright 2023 Smithsonian Institution. Reprinted with permission from Smithsonian Enterprises. All rights reserved. Reproduction in any medium is strictly prohibited without permission from Smithsonian Institution).
5 Zheng Ye et al., "Brain Imaging Evidence for Why We Are Numbed by Numbers", *Scientific Reports*, 10 (2020), 9270 <https://doi.org/10.1038/s41598-020-66234-z>
6 Michael Cavna, "Pixar Tips: 'Brave' Artist Emma Coats Shares her Storytelling Wit and Wisdom on Twitter (#FollowHer)", *Washington Post*, 25 June 2012 <https://www.washingtonpost.com/blogs/comic-riffs/post/pixar-tips-brave-artist-emma-coats-shares-her-storytelling-wit-and-wisdom-on-twitter%20followher/2012/06/25/gJQADaxd2V_blog.html> (accessed 9 November 2022)
7 Sarah Koenig, "The Alibi", Serial, podcast, 2014 <https://serialpodcast.org/season-one/1/the-alibi> (accessed 8 June 2023)
8 Jonathan Gottschall, *The Storytelling Animal: How Stories Make Us Human* (New York: Mariner Books, 2012)
9 John Yorke, *Into the Woods: How Stories Work and Why We Tell Them* (London: Penguin, 2013)
10 <https://www.who.int/europe/news-room/feature-stories/item/coping-with-the-unknown—a-family-s-story-of-living-with-long-covid> (accessed 2 August 2023). This excerpt is used with the kind permission of the WHO Regional Office for Europe.
11 Theodore A Rees Cheney, *Writing Creative Nonfiction: How to Use Fiction Techniques to Make Your Nonfiction More Interesting, Dramatic, and Vivid* (Berkeley, CA: Ten Speed Press, 1987)
12 <https://wellcomecollection.org/articles/YnjucxAAACIAHaFw> Licensed under a CC BY 4.0 international licence: <https://creativecommons.org/licenses/by/4.0/> (both accessed 2 August 2023)
13 Theodore A Rees Cheney, *Writing Creative Nonfiction*
14 Lee Gutkind, *Keep it Real: Everything You Need to Know About Researching and Writing Creative Nonfiction* (New York: WW Norton & Company, 2008)
15 Jessica Abel, *Out on the Wire: The Storytelling Secrets of the New Masters of Radio* (New York: Crown Publishing Group, 2015)

16 This story is based on Leo Babauta's blog post about killing email: <https://zenhabits.net/killing-email-how-and-why-i-ditched-my-inbox/> (accessed 2 August 2023)

17 Nora Ephron, "What Narrative Writers Can Learn from Screenwriters", in *Telling True Stories: A Nonfiction Writers' Guide*, ed. Mark Kramer and Wendy Call (New York: Plume, 2007) pp. 98–100

18 <https://humanparts.medium.com/how-i-became-a-dog-person-162ccfdc098e> (accessed 2 August 2023)

19 Ilia Gurlyand, "Reminiscences of A. P. Chekhov". *Teatr i iskusstvo*, 28:11 (1904), 521

20 Elizabeth Weil, "You Are Not a Parrot", *New York Magazine*, 27 February 2023 <https://nymag.com/intelligencer/article/ai-artificial-intelligence-chatbots-emily-m-bender.html> (accessed 31 May 2023)

21 For the latest view on how technology impacts writers, consult a professional organisation such as the Society of Authors (in the UK) or the American Society of Journalists and Authors.

22 William Zinsser, *On Writing Well: The Classic Guide to Writing Nonfiction* (New York: Harper Perennial, 2016)

Part II

Developing online and audio stories

4 Storytelling with purpose

This chapter prompts you to consider why you write stories and what's special about you as a writer. It explores the challenges and rewards of telling your own story and explores questions around story ownership. The chapter covers:

- Your brand values and writing purpose
- Story takeaways
- Sharing your own story and public narrative
- Checking that it's your story to tell
- Using stories to advocate for change

On American Independence Day 2012 R&B singer Frank Ocean posted a story about his first love on Tumblr.[1] Ocean's post highlights one of the reasons that people choose to tell stories online: to share their own story in their own way.

In Ocean's story, he meets someone and spends an entire summer with them, only to discover that his feelings aren't reciprocated. Though Ocean made no direct statement about his sexuality, it's clear that the "someone" in his story is a man. Sharing this information on social media was an unusual move at the time. Many celebrities didn't talk about their sexuality in public; those that did usually came out via mainstream media.

Just two days before Ocean posted his story, American soccer player Megan Rapinoe stated in an interview with *Out* magazine, "for the record: I'm gay". Ocean, on the other hand, circumvented traditional media. He controlled how his story was told and chose not to label himself. By writing and publishing his story on his own terms, Ocean was seen by some as a community builder.[2] For British rapper and radio host Dotty Charles, Ocean empowered a generation of queer musicians to be comfortable with their sexuality – to exist, says Charles, "unapologetically".[3]

DOI: 10.4324/9781003363347-6

Whatever your own motivation for writing, this chapter helps you think about who you are as a writer, how you write, and the impact you'd like your stories to prompt.

Why purpose matters

Every story won't have the impact of Ocean's, especially if it isn't shared by a celebrity. And every story doesn't need to change the world. But it's still worth thinking about what you want your stories to achieve. If you write a story without a purpose, you'll achieve something – a good story will, after all, involve and entertain people. But take time to identify your goals and you'll be able to shape your story to deliver the impact you want. Defining your purpose has other benefits too. It can help you to:

- Make consistent and impactful choices about story subjects, angles, and tone.
- Categorise stories so they may be found online, by selecting appropriate hashtags and search-engine keywords.
- Craft appropriate calls to action.
- Set a benchmark against which to evaluate your success.

Just as readers and listeners consume stories for many different purposes, you may write for a range of reasons, including to:

- Entertain or inform.
- Share your own truth in your own way.
- Make sense of your own experience.
- Surface unheard voices or reveal unseen perspectives.
- Raise awareness of an issue or advocate for change.
- Connect with others or share experiences others will identify with.
- Persuade someone to do something, like share, subscribe, visit a website, or spend money.
- Build a community or establish an online following.

Many writers aim to achieve several of these. For instance, podcaster King Kurus tells stories to entertain, to inform, and to give due respect to the people whose little-heard stories he shares.

In practice: telling stories that matter (*Black History Buff*)

The *Black History Buff* podcast grew out of love. When writer and host King Kurus's son was three years old he became, as Kurus puts it, "colour aware". Facing questions about what it meant to be Black, Kurus asked himself, how do I teach a three-year-old about slavery and oppression? Ashamed of that first instinct, Kurus set out to help his son build a positive self-image. As a first step, he made the study of Black history and Black culture a priority in his home.

Kurus allowed his son to see him studying Black history books and bought his son a book of his own. A year later, his son told Kurus about Marcus Garvey after reading about the Jamaican political activist in this book. Kurus then created a resource of positive stories for others. He posted these on social media and started the *Black History Buff* podcast.

The show didn't just grow out of love, it became a labour of love. Kurus has dyslexia. He failed English at school and mistakenly thought making a podcast wouldn't involve writing. He soon realised, "all I do is write". Kurus persisted because podcasts enable him to talk freely and to tell stories with sound – at least as soon as he had taught himself how to edit audio.

Entertainment and honour

On one level, the show delivers entertainment. Kurus describes it as a "fun and thrilling" journey through the African diaspora, a journey that spans continents and millennia. Episodes feature everyone from the first Black American to be awarded the Navy Cross to German-born Miss Lala (known as the "iron jawed acrobat") and a Queen who ruled part of present-day Sudan over 2,000 years ago.

Look past the history and entertainment, though, and you'll find a deeper purpose. While information about people featured in the show may be found in other sources, Kurus feels they haven't been, "placed on the pedestal they should have been placed on". The podcast reveres and honours them like historical figures who have been memorialised with statues. This purpose drives Kurus to spend hours researching, scripting and presenting stories alongside his day job. For Kurus, it's worth the time if someone listens to a story about a person they've never heard of and thinks, "this person's life matters".[4]

What you write about and why influences how readers and listeners perceive you. If you always write stories calling for action to address climate change, you'll become known for that. If you regularly draw on an encyclopaedic knowledge of 1960s Bollywood musicals, you'll become known for that. If every story you write ends with a call for readers to take care of themselves, you'll be known for that. Your reputation is shaped by what you write about, how you write, and how people feel about you. All these elements combine to create your author brand.

The value of brand

When we think of strong brands – like Apple, Nike, or Disney – we tend to picture their logos or slogans. These are tangible representations of a brand, but they're not the brand itself. A brand is built up from who you are, what you do, how people perceive you, and how people relate to you. Apple fuels its brand with sleek product design, straightforward marketing content, hyped product launches, and a focus on customer experience. Together, these create a strong emotional connection between Apple and its customers.

Companies like Apple understand the *value* of brand. They invest in their brand and measure success by brand awareness and loyalty. In comparison, as an individual writer, a brand may feel unnecessary. Yet people reading or listening to your stories draw conclusions about who you are anyway. Everything you do – the stories you choose to tell, the language and tone of your writing, the visual layout of your story, the sound design of your podcast – sends a message about who you are and what matters to you.

If you're writing for a client, brand will matter to them too. Some organisations develop detailed brand guidelines that demonstrate how to write in their preferred voice. If you find yourself working with a client who hasn't documented their brand, you'll need to ask questions to uncover what they value, how they work, and how they connect with customers or users. This can be a time-consuming process – so much so that I build a short brand-defining stage into the start of many client projects. Clients don't usually expect this, but they always appreciate it. Time spent answering my questions is time saved in revisions, because I'm able to write copy that supports how they want to be viewed.

Developing your author brand

Think for a moment about the people you follow on social media. They might be ordinary people, writers, musicians and actors, celebrities, companies you've purchased items from, or individuals with shared interests or similar lived experience. Why do you follow *these* people and not others? While some may share useful or interesting information, you probably identify with these people's values and value a relationship with them. Perhaps you follow a news organisation because you align with its political stance. Perhaps you follow a celebrity because they feel like the big sister you never had.

Now think about why people choose to follow *you*. What's important to you? And what's important to your readers and listeners? People might identify with your background, your experience, or your attitude. They might be drawn to your political leanings, a commitment to sharing the stories of marginalised individuals, or a belief that everyone should be valued in the workplace, no matter their background. Your brand doesn't need to represent everything about you, but it should reflect a slice of your life and personality. To work out which slice you'll share, you first need to get to know yourself.

In practice: getting to know yourself

Find a quiet space where you won't be interrupted and spend a few minutes jotting down answers to these questions.

1 How do you spend your free time?
2 What skills do you have?
3 What's special about your personality?
4 What do you know about?
5 What do you care about?
6 How do other people describe you?

You may represent your responses as a mind map if you like. Whether writing or sketching out your responses, these tips can help you get the most of out of this exercise.

• Be honest. This isn't about impressing anyone or about downplaying your strengths. If you struggle with a question, ask a trusted friend or colleague for their view.
• Bear in mind that "skills" and what you "know" can be almost anything. Don't feel that you need to be serious or academic. Perhaps you have the skill of being able to recite every Avengers movie, word for word. Or maybe you always know where to buy the best decaffeinated coffee in every city you visit.
• Be specific. You might watch Netflix in your free time, but what sorts of shows or films do you spend most of your time watching? You might care about social justice, but which injustice riles you the most?
• Don't worry about putting the right answers under the right headings, just try to document all the different aspects of what makes you you.

Now look back at your answers. Take a highlighter and select:

1 The specific skills, knowledge and passions that influence what you write about.
2 The specific aspects of your personality that influence your writing style.
3 Any answers that influence what you want to achieve in your writing.

These are the basic components of your brand – the things that make you and your writing unique.

Overall, what do you think makes you special? Why will your stories differ from those told by someone else? This specialness may come from your specific knowledge, your lived experience, or a deep-rooted passion. It may be an unusual combination of things, or it may be special simply because of the context in which you write. For instance, I have a science background, something that's not special in and of itself. However, it *is* special within the sectors in which I work (publishing and museums), which are more commonly populated with arts graduates. This sets me apart from most of my clients and collaborators.

Your brand values

Once you have an idea of "who" you want to share with readers or listeners, you can move on to identify the "how". How you write is influenced by what matters to you. Think about how you live your life, how you interact with others, and how you'd like to be perceived.

In practice: defining your values

Take a piece of paper and split it into two columns. Title one column, "I'm this", the other, "I'm not this". Place each of these words in whichever column sounds right. Add other words to either column if you like.

cool   down-to-earth   cutting-edge   wise   innovative   conservative   professional   empowering   formal   eclectic   savvy   informal   trendy   casual   approachable   spiritual   spontaneous   supportive   curious   balanced   compassionate   fun   funny   expert   well-informed   creative   determined   open   self-effacing   diligent

Scan down the "I'm this" column and highlight any words you'd like people to say about you when they read or listen to your writing. These words sum up your writing brand values. They'll be useful when you come to make decisions about story angles and writing style.

You'll build the strongest connections with readers and listeners who share your values and have a similar personality. That's why organisations like Innocent Drinks write stories that sound as if they're being recounted by a friend.

In practice: connecting with customers through story (Innocent Drinks)

From its launch over two decades ago, smoothie manufacturer Innocent has told stories on its product packaging. Written in a chatty, wacky style, this "wackaging" immediately built connections with customers. "The more stuff we wrote", says Innocent Head of Brand and Creative Dan Germain, "the more people got back in touch with us".

Today, stories are displayed on the Innocent office wall, shared on social media, and published on innocentdrinks.co.uk. "Everywhere," explains Germain, "there's a bit of a story". Even after 20 years, lines like, "stop looking at my bottom" (printed on the underside of Innocent drink cartons and gracing the foot of its website) set the brand apart.

Innocent origin stories

Visit the "a bit about us" page on Innocent's website and you'll find two versions of the company's origin story – one short, one long. In just 169 words, the short story reveals that Innocent was born from a desire to make it easy for people to do themselves some good. After testing the smoothie concept at a music festival and launching the business, the story ends with a transformation: Innocent's mission today focuses on keeping the planet healthy and supporting in-need communities.

The long version of the origin story comprises 83 individual moments spanning 21 years. Some are masterclasses in short storytelling, like moment number 9, in which one of the founders shakes his smoothie bottle while hungover. Unaware that he had removed the cap from the bottle, he spills it everywhere and Innocent gain a pithy new piece of label copy: "shake before opening (not after)".

Elsewhere on the website, you'll find a story about Innocent's efforts to increase the proportion of recycled plastic within its bottles and a story about Innocent's approach to diversity and inclusion.

Embodying Innocent

Every Innocent story is written in a natural, warm voice. The founders say they talk to customers like they talk to one another and their friends. For Germain that's, "dumb … a bit rubbish", but interesting and funny. Whether Innocent's tone works for you or not, the company's consistent storytelling in a human voice reinforces its number one value. Above all, Innocent culture is about being yourself, speaking openly and treating others as you'd like to be treated – all aspects that shine through the company's stories online and on package.[5]

Story takeaways

If your purpose involves raising awareness or prompting action, you'll need to think about what your reader or listener takes away from your stories.

Imagine you were aiming to sell something. You (or your client) would want a reader or listener to take away messages like this:

1 This is a great product.
2 I need this product.
3 I need to buy it now.

I've ordered these takeaways in a numbered list because they need to occur to the reader or listener in this order too. There's no point communicating the need to buy a product *now* if your potential customer doesn't understand what the product is or hasn't realised it might be useful.

Thinking about story takeaways can help you make decisions about your story angle and your story structure (aspects that we'll explore in more depth in Chapter 5). If you find yourself overwhelmed with takeaway messages, don't try to cram them all into one story. Instead, write multiple stories that each prompt a separate action.

Your purpose statement

With your brand components and values in mind, and what you want your readers or listeners to take away, you can now identify what your writing might offer a reader or listener and why it would interest them. As we saw in Chapter 1, people read and listen for a whole range of reasons, including wanting to be:

- Informed
- Inspired
- Entertained
- Educated
- Connected
- Supported
- Helped

Which of these would motivate someone to read or listen to one of your stories? Try to choose just one main answer, even if other motivations apply too. Now look back at your responses to the earlier exercises in this chapter and draft a purpose statement for your writing. A "purpose statement" is a sentence that summarises what you'll write about, who you're writing for, and why they'll want to read or listen to your writing. It's expressed in this form:

I tell stories about X for Y so they can Z

For example, you might say:

I tell stories about women making a positive difference in the world **for** young women who care about equality **so they can** be inspired to take action themselves or

I tell stories about my experience as an international student **for** other university students **so** they can feel part of a community of people with similar experiences

When drafting a purpose statement, it's sometimes difficult to come up with the last line – the reason anyone will read or listen and what they'll gain from the experience. To get to the root of your offer revisit your takeaways. If you're still stuck, try drafting a few different statements and reflect on which feels right. Share them with friends or colleagues too, asking which makes most sense, which piques their interest, and which feels most authentic to you.

Keep your purpose statement in mind when you select which stories to tell and while you write. Use it to create your writing byline, website bio, and social media profile. Refer back to it when you edit your work, so you can ensure your writing is "on brand".

Sharing your own story

Some writers achieve their purpose by writing stories about other people. For many, though, their goals are best achieved by sharing their own life experiences. The act of sharing your own story may benefit you as much as your audience. It can help you make sense of a challenging time or recognise what you've achieved. It can validate your experience, open up connections with others, and empower you to live differently in the future. Of course, sharing an authentic story involves opening up about your life, including aspects you might usually avoid talking about, as Rachel Bruce's experience shows.

In practice: sharing the whole truth (Rachel Bruce)

As a professional publisher, Rachel Bruce has spent years advising people to write with their audience in mind. Yet, when she shared her own deeply personal story about watching her mother die, Bruce ignored the people who would read it.

After discovering that her mother had advanced kidney cancer, Bruce – who describes herself as, "an unlikely runner" – began running. Two months after her mother died she ran the London Marathon to raise money for the hospital where her mother was treated. When she later spoke at briefings for other fundraising runners, Bruce was honest about her limited running experience, but she didn't reveal the whole story.

"You tell your story in whatever way you want", Bruce says today. And at those talks, where she mingled with athletic-looking runners over drinks and nibbles, Bruce didn't want to be seen for what she was: someone who, as she later wrote, dealt with her grief by "self-medicating with alcohol". This omission left Bruce feeling like an imposter. So, when she was asked to write about her experience for the hospital website, she wanted to reveal more. The result is a raw, vulnerable story about her mother's illness. It involves Bruce's journey with running *and* her relationship with alcohol.

Getting to the truth

Bruce's first drafts were packed full of adjectives and adverbs. She quickly realised that these obscured the truth, so she stripped everything back. She focused on facts and used, as she puts it, "honest, brutal language". One of the story's most striking lines, repeated several times, is, "I ran. I looked after my mum. I drank".

The secret to writing such a candid story is, says Bruce, to "forget about your audience". She forced herself to stop worrying about what people would think of her. She questioned every sentence. She removed anything she'd written to impress, to make the story more interesting, or to hide the truth. Noticing that she'd toned down the pivotal moment in the story (and a pivotal moment in her life), because her children might one day read it, Bruce chastised herself. She rewrote the passage to reveal what really happened. This drive came from Bruce's purpose: she wanted to write a complete and honest account of how she really felt and how she dealt with her grief.[6]

Telling stories about yourself brings many additional challenges, not least the emotional demands of reliving traumatic experiences and revealing vulnerabilities. For Bruce, writing about her mother's death brought everything back. Even when she re-reads her story today (years later), the emotions return.

If you're considering writing stories about your own lived experience, these tips can help you stay on track, while taking care of yourself.

- **Be selective.** Because you know the subject of you inside out, it's tempting to share everything. If you know you want to write about your personal experiences but aren't sure which specific moments to write about, spend some time mapping out your life. Look for turning points that might become events in a story: moments of challenge, collaboration, or transformation. A popular way to do this is to depict your journey through life as a river, complete with meanders around rocks, tributaries, rapids, and waterfalls.[7]

- **Believe in the power of your story.** Believe that your story can make a difference. Don't censor yourself because you think you don't have a story to tell or because no one will be interested. As writing coaches Heather Box and Julian Mocine-McQueen say, even if you only reach one person, "your story can always change someone's life". [8] And if *you* don't tell your story, someone else just might.

- **Be authentic.** Show your vulnerability and your personality. If you don't, readers and listeners won't connect or empathise with you. Don't shy away from difficult or challenging moments either. Share them if they're integral to the story, and so long as you feel able to.

- **Take care of yourself.** Recognise that opening up about your experiences may bring up intense emotions. Set boundaries and stick to them. Only share what you're comfortable talking about and what you don't mind other people knowing. Seek out people who can provide emotional support while you're writing.

- **Take care of others.** While it's useful to temporarily forget about your readers and listeners so that you don't self-censor, remember that you're writing for real people. Be aware of how your story may affect others. Consider what impact this could have on other people and whether you're OK with that.

- **Start small.** Test out sharing your story by telling it to people you trust. Share snippets on social media, with friends or family. Notice how you feel afterwards. Try the finished version out on someone you trust before you publish it to the world.

- **Ride the creative rollercoaster.** As with any creative project, writing about yourself can feel like riding an emotional rollercoaster. At the start, you're full of nervous anticipation, excited about what may come. As you wrestle out a first draft you feel scared and despondent. You start to question your work. You question yourself. But stick with it. What sets successful writers apart from people who never finish a story is their resilience. If you can weather the most daunting part of the process, you'll emerge with hope that everything might turn out OK. As you revise your writing and share it with others, you start to feel more confident. Finally, at the end of the ride you'll feel, as Rachel Bruce did, a sense of accomplishment and pride.

- **Be prepared for the public response.** If people connect with your experience they may see an opportunity to share their own experiences too. Be sensitive to any responses you receive, while taking care of yourself. Be realistic about the level of support you're able to provide.

Despite the challenges, telling your own story is rewarding. If the story describes overcoming adversity, you'll gain hope for a better future.[9] You may build connections with others and even drive change, as Josh Robbins did when he shared his story about testing positive for HIV.

In practice: an accidental advocate (Josh Robbins)

When Josh Robbins tested positive for HIV back in 2012, he didn't know a single other person with the same result. He felt scared and, as he wrote soon after, "didn't want to die". As someone whose face had been printed on posters campaigning for HIV awareness, Robbins wanted to be open about his status. He filmed his doctor giving him his test result and – two weeks later – bought the domain imstilljosh.com.

Robbins started a blog so he had a place to share the video. He shared his news authentically, sending a clear, positive message. His first post said:

"I'm Josh. I'm HIV Positive. So What? I'm Still Josh."

Within 24 hours the post had been viewed by 1,800 people. After seeing it, another man from the same small town in Tennessee made a video about his own HIV-positive status. More followed. The blog that started as somewhere for Robbins to share his own story evolved into a place where "Some of the posts are about me. Some are about news and activism related stuff. And other posts are written by some of my pals."

Though he never planned to be an activist, Robbins knows from his own experience that if you reach someone newly diagnosed, give them encouragement and wisdom from others living with HIV, and ask them to help, they will be "the greatest tool" in driving behaviour change. This purpose led Robbins to carry on writing and sharing stories.[10]

As Robbins highlights over a decade later, "I only spoke out because I could".[11] He wasn't in any danger and he had the freedom to choose whether to share his story. Many other people don't have the same opportunity. "It doesn't make me any better", says Robbins, "any more honest, or more notable than someone who didn't choose to share their own journey". Nevertheless, thanks to his writing, Josh Robbins became a leader of sorts. People identified with his experience and shared their own stories with him. Through his blog and social media activity he created a community of people who worried about the same things and cared about the same issues. This gave Robbins – and everyone else involved – far more power to call for change than if he had kept his story to himself.

Public narrative

Josh Robbins's journey – from telling his own story to creating a community and advocating for change – mirrors a process known as public narrative. Developed by Marshall Ganz at Harvard University, the public narrative framework inspires people to take action and call for change by linking personal stories with collective concerns. It is, according to Ganz, "an exercise of leadership", which motivates people who share your purpose to join you. The public narrative framework comprises three distinct elements that combine to tell one impactful story: the story of self, the story of us and the story of now.[12]

Story of self

Everything starts with an individual's lived experience and the story of self: a first-hand story that introduces the challenges that person faced, the choices they made and the outcomes their choices led to. The story of self identifies why someone wants to see a change in the world and why they – personally – are asking for it.

For example, five years after his positive test, Josh Robbins wrote a story about the struggles that he faced navigating and accessing healthcare as an HIV-positive gay man. The story described several challenging events, the impact these had, and what Robbins did in response. For instance, Robbins was:

- Dropped by four different health insurance companies, but fought to get new insurance cover.
- Instructed to order medicine from a specific pharmacist, but insisted on continuing with the pharmacist who knew about his allergies.
- Not treated as an individual, but he found a new doctor who listened to his needs.

The story of self makes other people aware of a problem and its impact. It encourages people to care about the storyteller's experience, while revealing the values that led the storyteller to call for change. In Robbins's story, he emphasises his desire to be seen and heard. "Each of us", he says, "has the right and needs to be heard as an individual in our own personal healthcare".[13]

Story of us

The story of us links the story of self with a collective experience. If we imagine that, after his story about accessing equitable healthcare was published, Robbins was contacted by other people facing similar challenges, then he might have written a story of us that looked something like this: "When I told my story, another young man reached out to me. He told me about the difficulties he faced when dealing with health insurers and said he never felt heard by them. In the past six months I've met dozens of people who say they feel more like statistics than individuals."

The story of us has power because it builds a community of people with shared experiences and values and invites others to join. Sometimes this invitation is explicit. Sometimes people come together because they feel connected and want to be part of something. The "us" in the story of us can be a focused group of people (like HIV-positive men in the US) or a larger collective (like everyone around the world who struggles to access healthcare).

Story of now

The story of now sets out what specific change the community demands. Again, extrapolating from Robbins's initial article, he might then be able to write a story of now along these lines: "When I looked into the issue, I discovered that over X per cent of HIV-positive Americans say they don't feel heard in the health system. That's X,000 people denied their right to personal healthcare." Stories like this often end with a call to action. In Robbins's initial story he himself concluded "I will be heard. You should be heard as well. Let's fight to make it happen."[14]

The story of now builds on the emotional connections forged by the stories of self and us. It articulates the urgent actions needed to achieve the community's goals and invites people to make actionable commitments to change. The focus shifts from the challenges people face to the positive: the positive change needed in the world and the positive outcome that comes from working together.

Public narrative is used by many different types of individuals and communities, from business leaders and politicians to people with lived experience of health conditions or facing health inequalities. What unites them all is a desire to make change happen – and the ability and freedom to share their story.

Is it really your story to tell?

Thinking about your purpose can help you sense check whether you should be telling a story in first place. As writer Ijeoma Oluo points out, sometimes telling your story may prevent others from telling theirs.[15] Sometimes what we view as "our story" really belongs to someone else; we choose to tell it only because society has made us feel we're somehow better at telling it. For writer Rebecca Solnit, questions like who your story is about, who matters, and who decides are "one of the battles of our time".[16] As a writer, you have the power to tell stories. You also, as Solnit points out, have the power to intervene in societal imbalances, amplifying others' voices over your own.

To weigh up whether to tell a story or not, ask yourself these questions, which are based on prompters shared by Ijeoma Oluo:

- **Is this my story?** Did it happen to me? Was I the main person involved? Will sharing it affect me more than anyone else?
- **What would the story look like if I told it from someone else's viewpoint?** Can I share my perspective without denying other people's experiences and perspectives? As writer Chimamanda Ngozi Adichie says, if you start "with the arrows of Native Americans, and not with the arrival of the British" you end up with an entirely different story – one which controls how people interpret history.[17]

- **Do I have more power or privilege than other people in the story?** If I do, will telling the story empower or disempower others? Am I speaking for someone with less power and privilege?
- **Do I care about how this will impact other people?** Should I care about these people's views?
- **What do I want to accomplish?** Am I writing for personal gain? Could I find ways to amplify others' voices?

One common story type that would struggle if passed through this list of questions comes from the field of charity fundraising. In the past, many charities in the Global North told stories of aid workers or donors visiting communities in the Global South. Aiming to build a bridge between the people receiving aid and the people being asked to fund it, these stories highlighted the problems that local communities faced, but showed them through the eyes of these benevolent overseas visitors.

Stories like this don't reflect reality, since many development aid workers come from the communities receiving aid. They may also, as Dr Chinonso Emmanuel Okorie and Lindis Hurum state in a Medecins Sans Frontieres (MSF) video calling out the organisation's former fundraising approach, "propagate a single story and perpetuate racist stereotypes of so-called white saviors and powerless victims". In the future Okorie and Hurum say they want to "pass the mic" to colleagues around the world to show a more representative picture of who MSF is.[18]

At the end of the MSF video, Okorie and Hurum question whether donors will give money to people who don't look like them. Yet research suggests, moving away from traditional fundraising stories like this may have a positive impact on charitable donations.[19] In the case of non-governmental organisation Amref, stories created by the communities receiving aid had greater impact – for both readers and writers.

In practice: telling a community's story (Amref)

Amref partners with communities in 35 countries to strengthen health systems and improve access to life-saving care. Committed to ethical storytelling and representation in its fundraising and communications, in 2021 Amref sent two different types of stories to its supporters to investigate how potential donors would respond.

One story followed Amref's usual approach. It opened with a letter from the Amref CEO, included professionally shot photographs, and included facts about the impact of donating money. It ended with a clear call to action, encouraging supporters to "play your part" in making a difference.

The other story was developed by Patrick Malachi, a community health worker (CHW) in the Kibera neighbourhood of Nairobi. As part of the research project, Malachi and other CHWs attended a five-day workshop to learn about fundraising, storytelling, and photography. Malachi took his own photographs for a story about his community, wrote headlines, and collaborated with a designer to lay out the finished product. Written in an emotional tone, Malachi's story shows how much he cares about the wellbeing of the elderly people featured in the story.

After Malachi's and Amref's stories were printed and posted to supporters (with one story going to half, one going to the other half), Malachi's story raised the most money. It brought in 38 per cent more donations than previous Amref campaigns too.

Supporters who received Malachi's story said they:

- Connected with the story on an emotional level.
- Thought it was different from other appeals they see.
- Were happy that Malachi was making an active contribution, helping himself and his community.
- Felt the story was accurate, personal, and real.

Along with learning skills like photography, Malachi and the other CHWs who developed stories said they:

- Enjoyed being in control of the story and delivering an authentic story.
- Felt responsible for the people whose stories they told, and proud to communicate their community's story.
- Found it easier to gain consent to take community members' photographs.

Malachi himself stated, "I feel appreciated that we came with a story about my community, I am the one who developed a story, rather than the world telling my stories."[20]

Stories like Patrick Malachi's are impactful because they show people making an impact on a major problem. They reveal a different side of the story to fundraising campaigns of the past, and give people hope that the world's problems can be solved. They tell a familiar story, but in a new way, by selecting a fresh angle that resonates with their intended audience. In the next chapter we'll find out more about choosing story angles, before exploring how to structure a story.

Summary

- Everything you do as a writer, from the stories you choose to tell, to the language and tone of your writing, sends a message about who you are and what matters to you.
- You'll build the strongest connections with readers and listeners who share your values and personality.
- Story takeaways summarise the key messages that you want readers or listeners to draw from a story.
- Sharing your own story can help you make sense of your experience, speak your own truth, raise awareness of an issue, connect with others, and advocate for change.
- Completing any creative project can feel like an emotional rollercoaster, even more so if you reveal something about yourself. Writers often feel nervous or excited at the beginning of the process, despondent in the middle, and confident and hopeful at the end.
- Public narrative is a process that inspires people to take action and call for change by linking personal stories with collective concerns.
- Sometimes what we view as our story really belongs to someone else. We may feel comfortable telling it because of societal norms, even if our action prevents others from telling their own story.

Practical lessons for online writers

- Define your author brand by selecting the slice of your life, personality, and values that you want to share with readers and listeners.
- Document your purpose by completing a purpose statement: I tell stories about X for Y so they can Z.
- Use your brand values and purpose statement to select appropriate stories and to check that you're writing "on brand". Encapsulate your brand and purpose in your byline, web bio, and social media profile.
- If telling your own story, take care of yourself and of others. Set boundaries and stick to them, try out how it feels to share your story with trusted friends, and consider the impact your story might have on other people.
- Use your power as a writer wisely. Take care not to silence others. Intervene in power imbalances if you're able to. Amplify others' voices.
- When advocating for change, focus on the positive by telling stories of resilience and empowerment. Forge an emotional connection through shared values before issuing a call for action.

Recommended reading

Heather Box and Julian Mocine-McQueen, Julian, *How Your Story Sets You Free* (Chronicle: San Francisco, 2019) – concise and readable introduction to understanding your story and how to share it.

Notes and references

1 <https://frankocean.tumblr.com/post/26473798723> (accessed 2 August 2023)
2 Alex Jones, "Why Frank Ocean's Letter Still Matters", *Fader*, 12 October 2015 <https://www.thefader.com/2015/10/12/frank-ocean-letter> (accessed 17 May 2023)
3 Dotty Charles, "How Frank Ocean's Coming Out Changed the Landscape", *PRS for Music*, 22 June 2021 <https://www.prsformusic.com/m-magazine/features/how-frank-oceans-coming-out-changed-the-landscape> (accessed 17 May 2023)
4 King Kurus, "My Story" *Black History Buff*, podcast, April 2019 and personal conversation with King Kurus, 19 December 2023
5 D&AD, *The Story of Innocent Drinks*, online video recording, Vimeo, n.d. <https://vimeo.com/143354154> (accessed 6 December 2022); Don Germain and Richard Reed, *A Book About Innocent: Our Story & Some Things We've Learned* (London: Penguin, 2009)
6 Personal conversation with Rachel Bruce, 16 May 2023
7 This is known as the "River of Life" exercise. You can find instructions for completing it here: <https://onbeing.org/wp-content/uploads/2019/05/on-being-river-of-life-exercise.pdf> (accessed 2 August 2023)
8 Heather Box and Julian Mocine-McQueen, *How Your Story Sets You Free* (Chronicle: San Francisco, 2019)
9 Sadie F Dingfelder, "Our Stories, Ourselves", *Monitor on Psychology*, January 2011 <https://www.apa.org/monitor/2011/01/stories#> (accessed 17 May 2023)
10 <https://imstilljosh.com/my-hiv-story-exclusive-content-for-positivelite-com/>; <https://www.poz.com/blog/why-do-the-activism> (both accessed 2 August 2023)
11 Personal correspondence with Josh Robbins, May 2023
12 Marshall Ganz, "What is Public Narrative: Self, Us & Now (Public Narrative Worksheet)", Working Paper, 2009 <http://nrs.harvard.edu/urn-3:HUL.InstRepos:30760283> (accessed 19 May 2023)
13 Josh Robbins, "I Want to be Heard in My Healthcare", *POZ*, 21 September 2017 <https://www.poz.com/blog/want-heard-healthcare> (accessed 19 May 2023)
14 Ibid.
15 Ijema Oluo, "Whose Story is it to Tell?", *Behind the Book*, 16 November 2021 <https://ijeomaoluo.substack.com/p/whose-story-is-it-to-tell> (accessed 17 May 2023)
16 Rebecca Solnit, *Whose Story is This? Old Conflicts, New Chapters* (London: Granta, 2019)
17 Chimamanda Ngozi Adichie, "The Danger of a Single Story", online video, TED, 2009 <https://www.ted.com/talks/chimamanda_ngozi_adichie_the_danger_of_a_single_story/> (accessed 8 June 2023)
18 Medicins Sans Frontieres, "Anti-Racism: When You Picture Doctors Without Borders, What Do You See?", online video, 6 December 2022 <https://www.youtube.com/watch?v=8DFemg94ufU> (accessed 8 June 2023)
19 Swee-Hoon Chuah et al., "White Saviour Perceptions Reduce Charitable Donations" <https://ssrn.com/abstract=4342940> (accessed 31 July 2023)
20 Jess Crombie and David Girling, "Who Owns the Story? Live Financial Testing of Charity vs Participant-led Storytelling in Fundraising", Amref UK, March 2022 <https://amrefuk.org/news/2022/04/who-owns-the-story> (accessed 20 May 2023)

5 Constructing your story

This chapter helps you attract readers and listeners by finding a fresh and interesting story angle. It also demonstrates how to develop a structure that will engage and involve. The chapter covers:

- Finding your story angle
- Building suspense
- When to step outside the chronological order of events
- How to make a story outline

If you knew me as a child, you'd probably be surprised that I now make my living as a writer. At school, I paid more attention to maths and science than anything to do with words. At home, I built plastic Airfix models, played with Lego, or improvised at the piano. I rarely had a book in hand – unless it was a nonfiction title about space exploration or spycraft. By the time I graduated from university (with a physics degree), I rarely wrote more than a sentence at a time.

Today, I see my science background as a strength, but this wasn't always the case. At the start of my publishing career, colleagues constantly shamed me for flawed grammar and misplaced apostrophes. Years later, I still worry that my writing's not up to scratch. In the end, though, a youth spent analysing, building, and improvising things turned out to be pretty good preparation for a career as a writer. It gave me a fundamental but often overlooked writing skill: problem solving.

Writers solve myriad problems, from story selection and structure to tone of voice and word choice. Problems like this rarely have straightforward solutions. Writerly problem solving isn't like completing a jigsaw puzzle, a task that has a single, knowable answer. Writing feels more like crafting a patchwork quilt. You start with a rough overall goal and a range of possible components. You select which pieces to use, which to leave out, and which to put next to one another. You try out different combinations, see how they look,

DOI: 10.4324/9781003363347-7

and rearrange them. Finally, you stitch everything together to make a coherent whole. You solve the problem not by landing on "the right answer", but by plumping for one of the many available solutions. This chapter helps you tackle two key writing problems:

1 What your story's about.
2 How to structure it.

Neither has a single, definitive answer. Both may lead you to make multiple quilts …

Thinking about stories

If you're drawn to writing because you're good with words, you'll need to flip into a new mindset when you make decisions about the focus and structure of your story. This stage of the writing process has very little to do with words and a lot to do with experimenting and asking critical questions. For writer Ted Cheney this is the moment when you, "sit back and sift, shuffle, and stack".[1]

When I'm sifting and shuffling, I step away from my computer. I sit somewhere I wouldn't usually work and I read through all the notes I've gathered – notes about the person and topic I want to focus on, what happened and when. Divorced from my computer, I can't be tempted to waste time massaging words and sentences. Instead, I think about how a reader or listener might engage with the story (see Chapter 1 for information about reader and listener needs).

Defining the problem

A sensible approach when solving any complex problem is to break it up into constituent parts. A story problem comprises numerous individual problems. Some relate to your audience and purpose, such as: Why am I writing this story? and Who is this story for? – both aspects we've explored in earlier chapters. Many relate to choices about words and sentences – which we'll address in Chapter 6. In this chapter we'll focus on problems about how material is organised within the story, such as: Where should I start? What can I leave out? and Where does *this* go? The first organisational problem you need to solve, however, is How will I attract readers or listeners to my story?

If the person in your story is relatable and the challenge matters, you're off to a good start. Odds are that you'll be able to write some kind of story that grabs attention. However, the stories that attract the greatest attention are those that take a fresh look at a well-known topic or issue. Attention-grabbing stories raise important questions about the world. They do this through a well-chosen "angle".

Story angles

Once you have a story idea – perhaps a person or subject you want to write about, perhaps a brief from a client – you need to decide what your story might be about. I don't mean who you're writing about, what happens to them, or what topic you're exploring. I mean the *angle* you will take.

A story angle is a bridge between the reader or listener's world and the topic or world that you'll immerse them in. For example, here are two story topics, and a potential angle for each:

• Topic: Owning a dog. Audience: People who aren't interested in dogs. Angle: I begrudgingly got a dog because my daughter wanted one, but ended up loving it more than I could ever have imagined.
• Topic: Getting lost. Audience: People who live with anxiety. Angle: I had a panic attack when I got lost in the souk in Marrakesh, but embraced the opportunity to walk for walking's sake.

In each example, the angle transforms the story topic into something else. In both cases, the twist happens after the word "but". Story editor and podcast producer Robert Rosenthal encapsulates this transformation in what he calls a "focus statement",[2] a sentence that also includes a "but":

Someone does something because X, but Y

Finding your angle

Without a Y for your focus statement, you don't have an angle. The most compelling angles, as newspaper columnist Adair Lara writes, always include, "an element of surprise", something that grabs attention because it takes an unexpected slant on the subject.[3] To write with conviction and passion, that slant ought to come from your own personal experiences, the research you gather, and what interests you. Sometimes it will be influenced by the information you're able to source or the needs of your client. Either way, it should resonate with your audience.

If the Y doesn't come naturally, you can take deliberate steps to seek it out. For instance, if your story feels too familiar, look, says editor Jan Winburn, for "a close-up angle" on it.[4] Tell the story from an unexpected point of view or extend it beyond where it usually starts or ends. Try transforming it into something unexpected with one of these approaches:

• **Reveal.** Emphasise that the story has been overlooked.
• **Re-specify.** Show that the story isn't what people think it is.
• **Value-switch.** Present the story through an unfamiliar moral stance.
• **Call out.** Encourage people to take some responsibility for the story.
• **Transform.** Show that the story needs to be changed.
• **Activate.** Inspire people to change the story.[5]

If you don't already have a story concept, search for the unexpected in the everyday or unusual situations that turn out to be strangely familiar. Seek out puzzling people, parts of daily life you've never stopped to consider, or thriving subcultures you knew nothing about. Ask "Why is that like this?" or "Why do we do things in that way?", questions that prompted journalist Marc Fennell to develop the *Stuff the British Stole* podcast.

In practice: *Stuff the British Stole*

The idea for award-winning podcast *Stuff the British Stole* came to Australian journalist Marc Fennell when he visited the V&A Museum in London and saw a life-sized, mechanical wooden tiger mauling a model of a European soldier. Why, Fennell wondered, was this tiger now on display in a museum 8,000 km away from its original home.

Starting with the tiger, each episode of the show begins with an object where it's housed today. Fennell then attempts to solve the mystery of how the item ended up there. For Fennell, museum objects are doorways into a wider world. "If you pull back the threads of objects that sit in museums", he says, you reveal stories that say something about people who – like Fennell himself – also ended up where they are because of the British Empire. A show that, on the surface, talks about things in museums, is, in fact, a podcast about colonialism and its lasting legacy.

Fundamentally, Fennell hopes to reveal, "What makes us tick and why we've set up society the way we have". He chooses objects for the show by asking:

1 How interesting is the story of the object itself?
2 What does that story tell us about how we ended up with the world we have today?
3 What does it tell us about ourselves?

Overall, *Stuff the British Stole* takes a distinctly different angle to the stories most museums tell about objects they display. Instead of focusing on what the object is or what it does, Fennell focuses on how and why the object was removed from its original home, shipped halfway around the world, and put on display. It's a "this story isn't what you think it is" sort of angle, with a dash of "we played a role in this".[6]

If you already have some idea of your story, look beyond the facts, feeling for anything that reveals what it's really about. Shuffle through your research

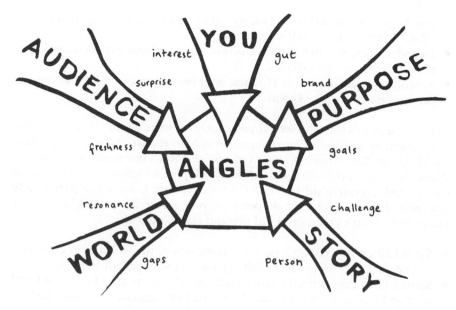

Figure 5.1 Routes towards story angles

and consider which corner of the topic you'll tackle. Looking for angles involves searching, and posing questions, in multiple places, as shown in Figure 5.1.

1 **The story itself.** What's most interesting or surprising about the person and their challenge? What motivated them? Where's the twist?
2 **Your purpose.** How might the story help me achieve my goals? Which aspects of the story align most strongly with my brand?
3 **You.** Which aspect of the story do I find most interesting and exciting? What does my gut say?
4 **Your audience.** Which aspect will my readers and listeners find most interesting, surprising, supportive, or inspirational?
5 **The world.** Which aspects of the story resonate most deeply with what's going on in the world? Is there a slant that could fill a gap in what's currently available?

To see how these routes work in practice, let's imagine that you want to write some kind of story about the development and use of Covid-19 vaccines in the early 2020s. Once you've completed some basic research, you start to think about the story itself and who it might be about – or whose point of view you'll tell the story from. Here are some potential people you might consider:

• Professor Sarah Gilbert from the University of Oxford, who led the team that developed the Oxford–AstraZeneca Covid-19 vaccine.

- Los Angeles nurse Kristen Choi, who participated in a clinical trial for the Pfizer–BioNTec Covid-19 vaccine.
- Ugandan nurse Judith Candiru, who visits local villages to provide information about Covid-19 vaccines.
- American grandfather Bob Hughes, who never got around to having the vaccine and contracted Covid-19.

Looking at this list, who would you choose to write about? If your purpose was something to do with encouraging people to receive the vaccine, perhaps you'd choose Bob Hughes's story. Otherwise, there's not much to go on yet. While there are obvious challenges (like developing a vaccine, recovering from Covid, and encouraging others to get the vaccine), none are particularly unexpected. If you dig a bit deeper with your research, you might discover more about what's going on. I did this and ended up with:

- Sarah Gilbert started work on the vaccine before the world even knew one was needed. One of her first challenges wasn't science, but funding.
- Kristen Choi experienced a rare bundle of side effects after her second trial dose and feared she had Covid. She worried that adverse reactions like hers would stop people from taking up the vaccine.
- Judith Candiru had Covid herself and was shunned by her local community. Today these people trust Judith so much they queue up to receive the vaccine from her.
- Bob Hughes ended up on a ventilator in intensive care. When he regained consciousness, he immediately asked his fiancée to get the vaccine.

Now, whose story would you choose to tell? Armed with this additional information, we can become more specific about the story challenges and craft potential focus statements. We can consider which we find most interesting or fresh, and which might appeal to our readers and listeners.

Personally, I'm most drawn to tell Sarah Gilbert or Judith Candiru's stories, with these angles:

1 As the Covid-19 pandemic spread around the world, Professor Sarah Gilbert started work on a vaccine (because she knew her team had the skills to make it happen), but didn't have enough funds to pay for the project.
2 Judith Candiru visits local villages sharing information about vaccines (because she wants to protect her community from Covid), but she was only able to do this once she had overcome the stigma of her own infection.

Both angles (the difficulty of gaining research funding for such a globally important project and the impact of stigmatisation in healthcare) feel fresh and unexpected. At the same time, they'll resonate with readers and listeners who have experienced related challenges (like not having enough resources to make something happen or being stigmatised for something totally beyond our control).

Personally, I'm attracted to these angles because I haven't seen either before. They also support my brand, because I want to tell stories about women who make a difference in the world.

Sense-checking your angle

While successful story angles are surprising, they also need to be understandable. Readers and listeners must "get" what the story is about and what's special about it. You, the writer, should be doing the hard thinking for them – researching and analysing information to make sense of the complexity of the real world. Here are two quick tests to check your thinking at this stage of the problem-solving process.

Test 1: write a story formula

Alex Blumberg, CEO of Gimlet Media, tests stories with what he calls the "story formula".[7] Like a focus statement, a story formula is another brief template with Xs and Ys:

I'm doing a story about X. And what's interesting about it is Y

The story formula forces you to identify why a listener or reader will care about your story. If you don't have a Y, your story may have all the necessary ingredients yet still fail to grab people's attention.

Test 2: share the premise

This American Life podcast host Ira Glass recommends explaining the basic premise of your story to a friend.[8] Consider how *you* felt while you talked it through (were you excited, bored, or confused?) and how *they* felt as they listened (did they understand it, did they ask you questions, did they continue talking about it afterwards?). "If you can't tell the story compellingly to a friend", says Glass, you haven't figured out what the story is really about.

Settling on an angle, says newspaper columnist Adair Lara, makes everything else easy, "because you know what to put in and what to leave out".[9] Yet, an angle is essentially a hypothesis – an idea about what your story will be like. As you complete more research, interview people, sketch out a structure and start writing, you may need to revisit the angle. At this stage, feel encouraged that you have a workable idea, but keep an open mind. If necessary, tweak the story as you develop it (though avoid any temptation to tweak it halfway through, else you'll end up with a story of two halves – each with different angles).

Structuring your story

The structure of your story is what keeps your reader or listener with you. It should grab attention at the start (by sharing information about a person and the challenge they face), build suspense (by setting out a well-chosen sequence of events that drives them on) and end with a resolution that ties up all the loose ends. The simplest approach is simply to tell the story chronologically, like this:

1 Introduce the person and the challenge.
2 Show the actions that the person takes while tackling the challenge (in chronological order).
3 Resolve the challenge and any loose ends.

You might hear this three-step approach described as a "Three Act Structure". Comprising a beginning, a middle, and an end, it's a simple story framework that's used again and again. Given its popularity, let's explore each part of this structure in detail.

Beginning: introducing a person

Your first scene should usually be presented from the perspective of the main person in your story. This might be someone who takes action or, particularly in podcasts, a narrator. Either way, this is the person who your readers and listeners will identify with, and the person whose point of view they follow through the story. The earlier you introduce this person and their challenge, the sooner readers and listeners become involved in their fate.

When we first meet someone in a story – particularly if they don't obviously feel like us – we may not immediately connect with them. Just like in real life, it can take a while to build rapport with someone new. In this case, you need a "save the cat" moment. In his book *Save the Cat!* screenwriter Blake Snyder describes this as a scene, "where we meet the hero and the hero *does* something – like saving a cat".[10] The save-the-cat scene demonstrates a key quality of the person in the story and encourages the audience to like them. If they would save a cat (or do whatever we focus on in this scene), we think, they must be thoughtful and kind-hearted. We therefore root for them.

Introducing any sort of character trait early on enables readers or listeners to use this knowledge later in the story. For instance, if you establish at the beginning of a story that someone is scared of heights, when you later write about them standing on the edge of a cliff, readers and listeners will automatically assume they're anxious – without you needing to spell it out.

In short-form stories, like those we see on social media or in blogs, this beginning section of a story is often extremely short. You may need no more than a sentence or two to identify who the story is about and introduce their challenge. You can then move on to how they overcome it.

Middle: building suspense

The middle of the story presents the sequence of events that show how the person responds to the challenge. Writers build up suspense, while readers and listeners become involved in what is happening.

Stories generate suspense when the reader or listener lacks knowledge about whether someone will overcome their challenge. This uncertainty fuels a desire to discover what happens. Even when we know the final outcome, we may still experience suspense, because we want to know *how* that outcome was achieved. Remarkably, even when we know an outcome *and* how it was achieved, we may still find a story suspenseful. This "anomalous suspense" occurs when we're so lost in a story that we ignore what we know *outside* the story and focus only on what we've been told *within* it.[11]

Readers or listeners experience high levels of suspense when they relate to a person, when the stakes are high (because the challenge matters), or when the possibility of the person overcoming the challenge feels increasingly unlikely. Some of the best ways to build suspense are outlined below.

- **Imposing a delay.** If you stretch out the time between when the challenge is introduced and when it is resolved, the reader or listener must wait to find out what happens.
- **Constraining the possible solutions to the challenge.** If you narrow the options available to the person in the story, the reader or listener will feel more anxious about whether they'll ever overcome the challenge. When there are – in reality – plenty of options, you'll need to distract readers and listeners by focusing their attention on other events. Like a magician's sleight of hand, this enables you to obscure a solution that was there all along.
- **Giving the reader or listener information that the person in the story doesn't have.** When readers and listeners know something someone in the story doesn't, it creates tension. For instance, if our heroine escapes from danger by running down a road that only *we* know is blocked, we'll start to worry about whether she'll be able to reach safety.
- **Beginning somewhere unexpected.** If the facts of your story are well known, radio scriptwriter Annie Caulfield suggests starting the story in a place "that makes it a challenge for you to reach the facts of the ending". This automatically intrigues your reader or listener. How, they will wonder, will you get from *this* starting point to *that* ending?[12]

Creating suspense is a careful balancing act. Whenever we read a story we expect some level of suspense. Without it we lose interest, but include too much and readers and listeners will walk away. They may end up feeling frustrated, bored, or even stupid (because they can't work out how the story might end).

End: resolving the threads

In the final section of a story, you release tension by revealing how the person overcomes the challenge. The resolution ties up all the loose ends of the story and signals to the reader or listener that this is, indeed, the end.

The end plays an important role in changing people's minds about an issue or in driving people to take action. Writing coach Bruce DeSilva describes the ending as "your final chance to nail the point of the story to the readers' memory so it will echo there for days".[13] Some storytellers do this more explicitly than others. For example, every episode of the *This American Life* podcast follows a standard structure in which an anecdote is followed by a reflection. Host Ira Glass likens this format to a sermon, in which the meaning of each story is made explicit. This meaning might be communicated by the narrator or by someone who has been interviewed within the story. Other writers leave it to readers or listeners to draw their own conclusions about what a story might mean.

Plotting your story

Chronological story structures are often the easiest to write and the easiest for readers and listeners to follow. After all, we're used to living life one event after another, so we feel comfortable with stories that do the same. However, there are occasions when it's helpful to move away from chronology. This might be because an ongoing, "this happened then this happened" sequence diverges too far from the reality of life. Alternatively, it may fail to build sufficient tension or it may feel too confusing.

To gauge whether a chronological structure makes sense, think about how someone coming to your story without any prior knowledge might react. Ask yourself:

- What are the main events that they need to know about?
- What will grab their attention and build the most suspense?
- Where might they become confused?

Ultimately, when plotting out your story, you're trying to solve the problem of "What does the reader or listener need to know, when?" Try to identify when your audience will ask questions like Who? Where? When? Why? and What happens next? Then select and arrange events to answer these questions. For instance, you might move an event towards the beginning of your story so that readers and listeners have a piece of knowledge that will help them make sense of a later event. Alternatively, you might delay revealing a vital piece of information until just before the end to keep the reader or listener in suspense.

To help solve the problem of what should go where, ask yourself:

1 **What does my reader or listener need to know at the start?**
   How will I set the scene?
   How will I introduce the main person in the story and the challenge they face?

What's the best way to get my reader or listener hooked?

Is there anything they need to know now, in order to understand what follows?

2 **Which key events will I share in the middle, in which order?**

What are the absolutely essential moments in the story (the key events that drive the action forward)?

What could I leave out without impacting the story?

What information could I hold back to build suspense?

What information do I need to reveal (or hint at) early on?

3 **How will I present the resolution?**

How do things end?

How will I demonstrate how the person in the story has changed?

What other loose ends need to be tied up?

What – if any – final point do I want to make?

If you do move events out of their natural chronology, be careful. You'll need to ensure that readers and listeners always understand where they are in the story. To avoid confusion in short-form writing, magazine writer Donna Baker recommends including no more than one flashback. Two or more are, says Baker, "dangerous".[14] They distract readers and listeners, who may then drop out of the story.

Trusting the story

One of the pitfalls of writing nonfiction is that writers collect vast amounts of information as they complete their research. There's a constant temptation to cram it all in, in order to show all your hard work. Resist this temptation! Only include what's required to involve your reader or listener and guide them through the story. If you do too much in a story, you risk losing readers or listeners. Even those who stick around may skip unnecessary material, as Wellcome Collection found when it developed and evaluated two media-rich digital stories.

In practice: Wellcome Collection stories

London's Wellcome Collection is a free museum and library exploring health and human experience. When the Museum opened its Reading Room gallery, the digital team commissioned two accompanying online stories. Each incorporated visual materials from Wellcome's collections. Like the gallery itself, the stories were designed for one key purpose: to deepen connections with the Museum's audiences.

I wrote one of these stories: a six-episode exploration of how and why people collect things. Along with text and images, the stories included video and audio material and specially designed graphic backgrounds.

For the episode about John Graunt, a merchant who lived in London in the 1600s, we created an interactive infographic. Graunt collected information about the causes of death of everyone who died in London, publishing his tabulations in a popular book. Our infographic enabled readers to explore this historical data through a visual interface. It included images and text that explained the nature of each deadly ailment documented by Graunt – from dropsy to plague.

Following publication, Wellcome studied the web analytics and evaluated the stories with users. The results showed that the stories achieved their overall goal: web visitors spent longer on this content than in other locations on Wellcome's website, while users said they felt interested and engaged in the stories. However, most users didn't make use of interactive elements like the Graunt infographic. In some instances, they felt overwhelmed or confused by them. Though the interactions were interesting, users found them distracting. They didn't want all this additional information, they simply wanted to focus on the story.

Today, Wellcome Collection still publishes stories online, but without all the extras that we included in those early examples. After experimenting with these, Wellcome evaluated what worked, and adapted its storytelling in response. This included creating episodic stories, after the evaluation highlighted the need to bring people back for more.[15]

Writers over-pack stories with extra information, sidebars, and features because they're suffering from what William Zinsser calls "definitiveness complex". It's a condition in which a writer feels compelled to produce the most comprehensive treatise on a topic. Its most dangerous side-effect is bloating. As the content expands, there's a serious risk of suffocating the story.

For Zinsser, focus is everything. Every successful piece of nonfiction should, he says, leave the reader with just one provocative thought. "Not two, or five – just one." If you realise that you've packed in too much information or too many story events, take a moment to question whether anything could be thrown out without affecting the story. Keep events that drive the action forward and stay focused on your angle. Use it like a sieve. It should let some ideas and information pass through, while keeping lumpy extras out of the story mix.

Developing a story outline

Once you have an angle, the structure of a story may flow naturally and you can simply start writing, making necessary adjustments as you go. In some situations, though, you might choose to write an outline or create a storyboard first – some kind of map that will guide you as you write. Outlines are particularly useful for long-form stories, episodic podcasts, and stories where the facts of the matter are too complex or convoluted to keep track of in your head. If you're working for a client, an outline delivers another benefit: it creates an opportunity to sign off your story concept, before you begin writing it.

Story outlines come in all shapes and sizes. Some are lengthy guides, typed up in minute detail. Others are brief lists scrawled on the back of an envelope. Pulitzer prize winner Jon Franklin writes outlines of just 15 words, even for stories that will be thousands of words long. Legendary journalist Gay Talese made elaborate colour-coded plans for his long-form articles.

Whatever style of outline you make, start by noting down what's essential to communicate at the beginning of your story and what you need to communicate at the end. Put your favourite events in the middle – moments that you feel simply *have* to be there. Then work out whether you need any additional scenes to help your reader or listener understand what's happening. If you'd mention specific scenes in a quick discussion about the story, they must be important – so include them.

As an example, let's see how I developed an outline for an online story commissioned by Lauderdale House, a historic building in north London. The brief called for short nonfiction stories (around 500 words) that would encourage visitors to find out more about the house's history. The client was particularly keen to reveal stories about women who had lived in or visited the house during its 400-year history.

One of the stories I chose to write centred around Arbella Stuart, a close cousin of King James I. When Stuart, who had a reasonable claim to the English throne, married William Seymour (who had a similar claim) in 1610, she and her husband were arrested. Soon after, Stuart spent six days at Lauderdale House, before later escaping custody to be with Seymour. There are many different versions of this story that might be told. In my case, my focus statement and story formula looked something like this:

- **Focus statement:** Stuart escapes from custody to be with her husband (because she loves him), but is re-captured and never sees him again.
- **Story formula:** I'm telling a story about Arbella Stuart and her struggles to be with the man she loved. And what's interesting about it is that women in some cultures experience similar challenges when their family doesn't sanction their choice of partner.

Based on my historical research, I listed out the most relevant events in chronological order. I usually do this in numbered lists of brief statements, but you could just as easily sketch everything out in a mind map.

1 Stuart and Seymour get married.
2 Stuart is put under house arrest.
3 Stuart and Seymour meet in secret.
4 Stuart is taken north.

5 Stuart falls ill and stays at Lauderdale House.
6 Stuart and Seymour meet while she is here.
7 Stuart escapes, dressed as a man, while staying at Barnet.
8 Stuart rides to Blackwall, by the river.
9 Stuart waits for Seymour, who doesn't appear.
10 Stuart leaves alone, on a boat bound for France.
11 Stuart is captured in the English channel.
12 Stuart is imprisoned in the Tower of London.
13 Stuart dies four years later.

When you see everything in a list like this, the story doesn't immediately sound compelling. What's more it looks long for a 500-word story. To create a more effective structure, I wrote each of these statements on a Post-It. Like a Hollywood filmmaker storyboarding a movie, this enabled me to test out different ways of revealing the story.

Whether you write, sketch, or arrange Post-Its to create your outline, it can help to think like a movie director. When directors develop and evaluate storyboards, they follow a number of rules of thumb. Two of the most important are:

- Every scene must serve a purpose.
- Only use jump cuts for dramatic effect.

If a moment or scene doesn't support the story you want to tell, cut it, however interesting you think it might be. If you're jumping from one part of the story to another too quickly for your reader or listener to follow your train of thought, incorporate one or more additional scenes to guide your audience through what's happening, or rearrange the scenes into a more logical order.

In my first Post-It outline for the Arbella Stuart story, I began with Stuart's marriage (which ought to have been a happy day, but sparked the misery to follow) and ended with her death – alone. I knew I had to include Stuart's stay at Lauderdale House (a requirement of the brief) and it was obvious that her escape from custody and her departure for France were important moments. These, therefore, formed the backbone of the story.

After evaluating this version of my outline, I decided to make two key changes:

1 Knowing that readers might need more explanation about why King James reacted to the marriage as he did, I decided to start with the death of the previous monarch (Queen Elizabeth I) and rumblings about Stuart's claim to the throne.
2 Given where the reader will be when they encounter the story (on the Lauderdale House website), I knew they would immediately question why the story was relevant, so I dropped some information about Stuart's stay into the start of the story.

Figure 5.2 A Post-It outline for a story about Arbella Stewart escaping from custody

When I pulled everything together, I ended up with eight distinct story moments, shown in Figure 5.2. In the final piece, some of these moments ended up as detailed scenes (mini-stories that have their own beginnings, middles, and ends), while some were covered in a sentence or two. Suspense builds in the middle, when Stuart takes action to achieve a goal, but is thwarted again and again.

The full list looked something like this:

1 Elizabeth I dies and is replaced by King James I, **but** some people think Stuart should have been installed on the throne. Eight years later she stays here at a pivotal time in her life.

2 Stuart marries Seymour, **but** then they are both arrested, because the King sees them as a threat.
3 The pair manage to meet in secret, **but** Stuart is ordered to be taken north. They may never see each other again.
4 Stuart begins her journey, **but** falls ill and stays at Lauderdale House. Here she sees Seymour for what might be their last meeting.
5 Stuart escapes while at Barnet (by dressing as a man) and makes it to the coast, where she waits for Seymour, **but** he doesn't appear.
6 Stuart leaves alone, on a boat bound for France, **but** is captured in the English Channel and imprisoned in the Tower of London.
7 Seymour makes it to France, **but** only returns after Stuart dies.
8 Stuart dies alone in the Tower.

Another writer might choose to focus on other events in this story (like how Stuart planned her escape, what life in the Tower of London was like, or what Seymour did after reaching Paris), so there's no "right answer" here. I settled on my version because it centred on the ups and downs of Stuart's efforts to be reunited with Seymour (consistent with my focus statement) and included moments (like the escape from Barnet) that highlighted the specific challenges faced by a woman (consistent with the story formula).

In the film industry, storyboards serve as templates for the filming process. Producers and directors refer back to them as they organise and shoot scenes in the film. In the same way, your outline is a framework on which to build your writing. Though you may end up diverging from it, an outline helps you focus on the events that matter. When it's complete, you're ready to tackle a new writing problem: how do I fuel readers and listeners' imaginations and bring my story to life? That's the issue we'll explore in the next chapter.

Summary

- A story angle is a bridge between the reader or listener's world and the topic or alternative world that you'll immerse them in. The most effective angles are understandable yet surprising. They resonate with their audience and say something insightful about the world.
- The simplest way to structure a story is to start with the person in the story and their challenge. Then arrange the events in the order in which they happened, before ending with the resolution of the challenge.
- Moving some events out of the natural chronology can help you gain readers' and listeners' attention, create suspense, or facilitate understanding.
- Too many out-of-order events, or any extraneous material, can jolt readers out of the story.
- Suspense is generated when readers or listeners lack knowledge about whether the person in the story will overcome their challenge.
- A story outline provides a framework for your writing and a sign-off point for client work. It helps you stay focused on the key information and events required to tell your story.

Practical lessons for online writers

- When you're working on angles and structure, shift your brain into a different mode. This might mean stepping away from your computer or working in a different location.
- Develop an angle before you structure or write your story. Use your research, your purpose, your understanding of your audience, and your personal take on an issue to home in on what makes the story fresh and meaningful.
- Use focus statements and the story formula to gauge whether you have an attention-grabbing story.
- Develop an outline that sets out what needs to go where. You can then use this as a template for the next phase of the writing process.
- Organise real-life events in a structure that guides readers through the action, while building suspense. Do this by holding back information or constraining the possible solutions to the challenge.
- Use flashbacks and flashforwards sparingly. If you must incorporate them, be sure to signal when you're moving readers or listeners back or forward in time.
- Trust your story. Don't be tempted to add in extraneous information or functionality.

Recommended reading

Mark Kramer and Wendy Call, *Telling True Stories: A Nonfiction Writers' Guide* (New York: Plume, 2007) – comprehensive collection of tips and tricks from a range of nonfiction writers, which includes sections on finding topics and constructing a structure.

William Zinsser, *On Writing Well: The Classic Guide to Writing Nonfiction* (New York: Harper Perennial, 2016) – one of my favourite books about nonfiction writing. A realistic, readable guide.

Notes and references

1 Theodore A Rees Cheney, *Writing Creative Nonfiction: How to Use Fiction Techniques to Make Your Nonfiction More Interesting, Dramatic, and Vivid* (Berkeley, CA: Ten Speed Press, 1987)
2 Rob Rosenthal, "In Focus: Ways to Home in on the Core of a Story", Transom, 25 May 2021 <https://transom.org/2021/in-focus-ways-to-home-in-on-the-core-of-a-story/> (accessed 13 February 2023)
3 Adair Lara, "Find an Angle to Bring Your Subject to Life", *Writer's Digest*, October 2010
4 Jan Winburn, "Finding Good Topics: An Editor's Questions", in *Telling True Stories: A Nonfiction Writers' Guide*, ed. Mark Kramer and Wendy Call (New York: Plume, 2007), pp. 22–4

5 These angles are adapted from a list shared in this article: Paul A Kramer, "How Narrative Journalists can Make "Good Trouble" to Tackle Social Problems", Nieman Storyboard, 6 December 2022 <https://niemanstoryboard.org/stories/reframing-narrative-stories-to-help-solve-societal-problems/> (accessed 1 June 2023)

6 Chris Dart, "Stuff the British Stole Host Marc Fennell Wants to Shake up Our 'Cultural Amnesia'", CBC, 6 January 2023 <https://www.cbc.ca/arts/stuff-the-british-stole-host-marc-fennell-wants-to-shake-up-our-cultural-amnesia-1.6704989> (accessed 10 January 2023); Meta, "Marc Fennell on Stuff the British Stole", Meta, 2 December 2020 <https://play.acast.com/s/meta/marcfennellonstuffthebritishstole> (accessed 10 January 2023) and TV Reload, "Marc Fennell Unpacks the Stuff the British Stole", TV Reload, 28 October 2022 <https://www.tvreload.com.au/episodes/episode/28586f4e/marc-fennell-unpacks-the-stuff-the-britsh-stole> (accessed 7 February 2023)

7 Alex Blumberg, "Alex Blumberg", Transom, 9 January 2005 <https://transom.org/2005/alex-blumberg/> (accessed 13 February 2023)

8 Ira Glass, "Ira Glass", Transom, 6 January 2004 <https://transom.org/2004/ira-glass/#story> (accessed 13 February 2023)

9 Adair Lara, "Find an Angle to Bring Your Subject to Life"

10 Blake Snyder, *Save the Cat! The Last Book on Screenwriting You'll Ever Need* (Studio City, CA: Michael Wiese Productions, 2005)

11 Richard J Gerrig, *Experiencing Narrative Worlds: On the Psychological Activities of Reading* (New Haven, CT: Yale University Press, 1993)

12 Annie Caulfield, *Writing for Radio: A Practical Guide* (Marlborough, Wilts: The Crowood Press, 2009)

13 Bruce DeSilva, "Endings", in *Telling True Stories: A Nonfiction Writers' Guide*, ed. Mark Kramer and Wendy Call (New York: Plume, 2007), pp. 116–21

14 Donna Baker, *How to Write Stories for Magazines: A Practical Guide* (London: Allison & Busby, 1986)

15 For more on this, see Danny Birchall and Anna Faherty, "Big and Slow: Adventures in Digital Storytelling", conference paper for *MW2016: Museums and the Web 2016*, 30 January 2016 <https://mw2016.museumsandtheweb.com/paper/big-and-slow-adventures-in-digital-storytelling> (accessed 7 June 2023)

6   Telling your story

This chapter helps you choose and arrange words to guide readers and
listeners through the Story Funnel – from gaining attention and forging
connections to transformation and action. It makes most sense to read
it once you have some idea (ideally an outline) of your story structure.
The chapter covers:

- Best practice for online writing
- Using tone to connect with readers and listeners
- Inclusive writing
- Sharing information
- Showing what happens
- Opening and closing your story

You've compiled all your story research, understood your brief (if you have
one), and reflected on what's likely to engage your audience. You have a story
purpose and topic, an angle, even an outline. You've completed, then, what I
call the "thinking" part of writing. Now you can get started with the "writing"
part of writing – the moment when you choose and organise words to tell your
story to readers or listeners.

When you embark on the writing stage, don't feel that you have to work
from the beginning to the end. Instead, focus on the most important moments
of the story first. You probably know these well and may have some idea about
how you'll present them.

Try to write your first draft without too much thought; just get the words
down. But if you realise that any section isn't working, don't keep trying to
fix it. Struggling to find the right words is often a symptom of a flawed structure. Stop fiddling with words, revisit your outline, and adapt it. Move events
around, insert an extra detail, or delete an entire section.

DOI: 10.4324/9781003363347-8

Unlike your structure – which most readers and listeners never notice – your words are visible or audible. They attract readers and listeners, make the story accessible to them, and build a relationship with them. Words help people build visual pictures of what's going on, so they can construct their own take on the story. In this chapter, we'll consider how words, sentences, and paragraphs do all this. While the advice is relevant to both online and audio formats, the specific challenges of writing for listeners are explored in greater depth in Chapter 7.

Before you get stuck in, check that you know:

1 **Who's narrating your story.** In nonfiction, this is often – but not always – you.
2 **Whose point of view you'll show the action from.** This is usually the main person featured in the story.
3 **Where you'll watch the action from.** Your vantage point might be in the thick of everything or you might relate events from a distance.

The answers to these questions may change at key points in the story, but they lay the groundwork for the tone you'll use, the detail you'll share, and your opening gambit.

Gaining attention through opening lines

Opening lines grab readers' or listeners' attention and give them, says writer Gary Provost, "something to care about".[1] The two most common approaches are to introduce a moment in time or to introduce an issue, as these examples illustrate.

> *Opening line 1*
>
> My brain is running around like a husky with the zoomies.[2]

> *Opening line 2*
>
> A theme of my life in Australia has been people telling me I don't belong here.[3]

The first example, from a story about writer Brooke Chang lying awake in bed due to stress, is a *moment-centred opener*, in which someone does something (in this case, Chang thinks one thought, then another, then another). Openers like this act like close-ups in films. They focus the audience's attention onto a person and a specific moment in their life.

The second example is an *issue-centred opener*, in which an idea, topic, or issue is introduced. Taken from a blog published on the website of ReachOut, an online safe space for young people, this opening sentence telescopes time to highlight the casual racism the author has experienced for most of her life. If you read on, you learn that Madhuraa Prakash moved to Australia from Sri Lanka when she was two; for 20 years she's been made to feel like an outsider in the place she calls home.

Surprising and provocative opening lines are particularly attention-grabbing. For instance, the final word in this opening sentence would leave most people wanting to know more: "My first panic attack was caused by holes". It's the intriguing beginning to a story about fear of monsters who appear almost human.[4] Alternatively, the line "It's hard to conceive of the idea of anonymity nowadays" shares an opinion. It gets us thinking about an issue and may prompt us to consider whether we agree with the writer. We're then primed to read the rest of this Art Institute of Chicago story about unknown makers of art (written by Paul Jones).[5]

There are, as William Zinsser points out, myriad options for how to start a story. "Anything will do", says Zinsser, so long as it nudges the reader or listener's curiosity, "and tugs at his sleeve".[6] Once that tug has gained your audience's attention, it's time to share your story – in the clearest and most involving way possible.

Writing for online and audio audiences

The number one priority when communicating in writing is clarity. With no opportunity to gauge how your words have been received, you must do everything you can to ensure you're understood. Readers or listeners shouldn't have to wade through unnecessary text to seek out vital information. Nor should they be left guessing about what's going on. Unfortunately, it's incredibly easy to bury information in turgid prose or churn out ambiguous statements. Clarity is achievable, though, so long as you make some smart decisions. These include:

- **Getting your thinking straight.** If you don't know your purpose and take-aways, key story moments, or what the subject is fundamentally about, you risk meandering around aimlessly. Some writers get their thinking straight before they type a word. Others – including me – use their first draft as an opportunity to disentangle all their thoughts. Only when they redraft are they able to focus on clarity.
- **Including only what your reader or listener needs in that moment.** Cram in too much and they'll find it difficult to take everything in.
- **Using as few, simple words as possible.** Don't hide information within forests of adjectives or behind redundant phrases. Only include a word or phrase if it advances the story.
- **Being specific and precise.** Choose appropriate words and eliminate every trace of ambiguity.

- **Introducing new ideas slowly.** Give readers and listeners time to absorb and understand everything. Aim to limit each sentence to just one idea, each paragraph to just one theme. Keep sentences below 25 words if possible.
- **Presenting events in the order in which they happen.** Like a news camera recording what's ahead of it, stay with the action, setting out each moment in turn. For instance, writing, "She opened the fridge. They were out of milk. She drove to the shop and picked up a bottle" is far easier to follow (and more elegant) than "She drove to the shop to pick up milk after she'd opened the fridge and seen there was none left".

To see how these tactics generate clear, precise text, let's take a look at a story written for Twitter (now X) by archaeologist and writer Electra Rhodes. In 1,100 words, Rhodes shares a story about her friend Pink and the bucket list he wanted to complete before he died. It's told through a series, or thread, of posts. Here are the first two. As you read, think about what information the writer included (and what she left out).

> It was six years ago, and my mate, Pink, had just been told he was going to die. He accepted the news with a grace I can only marvel at, but he said he'd a list of things he'd still like to do.
>
> We sat in a pub one night and read it over. Eight things? Four months? Ok. Deal.

> Don't get me wrong, he'd been pissed when he found out. Routine check up. Bit of a cough. Shadow on an X-ray. Bad. His wife had just had an all clear and it seemed particularly cruel.
>
> He told us when we were on a dig, heads in a trench, bums in the air. Dignified? Not.[7]

Rhodes skips over plenty of information in these posts. For instance, there's no backstory about how she and Pink met, because all we need to know is that they're mates. We never find out what disease Pink had, but that doesn't matter (because the story focuses on the bucket list, not Pink's health). Nor do we know exactly what was said in the pub. Again, that's unimportant.

When information does appear, it's shared in separate sentences, like so:

In post 1: Pink's diagnosis/the wish to do a bucket list/the discussion about it/the agreement to do it

In post 2: Where Pink was/why he went to the doctor/what the doctor found/Pink's wife's health/when Pink shared the news/what they were doing

Throughout, Rhodes uses simple words and short sentences. "Bad" is all we need to know about the diagnosis. The delightfully concise "Eight things? Four months?" sets out the goals and constraints of the challenge. "Deal" tells us that Rhodes agreed to help. These punchy sentences draw us into the action. We feel like we might be there with Rhodes and Pink too.

Unfortunately, few writers' first drafts look like this (mine included!). Replete with unnecessary words, complex terms, and vague statements, most writing could benefit from:

- Reducing clutter.
- Keeping things simple.
- Being precise.
- Writing to the format.

Let's look at each of these writing strategies in turn.

Reducing clutter

In his book *How to Write Short*, Roy Peter Clark devotes an entire chapter to the topic of dumping. "No dumping", says Clark, "is not a bad motto for how to write well on the Internet".[8] Sometimes writers throw in extra material because they can't bear to leave it out. Sometimes they clutter up their text with words that shouldn't be there.

When we begin paragraphs, sentences – or even simple phrases – it's human nature to engage in a written version of throat clearing. Like coughing before we speak, or rambling on before we get to the point, we start with words or phrases that add little to our copy. Just think how many times you've read or written phrases like, "he started walking across the room", "I remember thinking" or, "at this point she came to a realisation". Each is much improved when shortened (to "he walked across the room", "I thought" and "she realised").

What all these throat rumblings have in common is clutter: words or phrases that serve no purpose. Another common gathering place for clutter is around verbs and adjectives. Statements like "the restaurant mainly focuses on" or "she initially began" include unnecessary qualifiers (adverbs or other words that comment on a verb or adjective). Remove these and the writing improves (to "the restaurant focuses on" and "she began").

Unnecessary qualifiers aren't simply redundant; they get in the way. For instance, if you describe an object as "slightly unique" it's unclear whether the item is unique or not. If it *is*, then drop the "slightly" and stand firm with your claim. As William Zinsser puts it, "Don't be kind of bold. Be bold."[9] If the object you're describing isn't, in truth, unique, choose another word. "Strange", "extraordinary", "idiosyncratic", or "rare" might each do a better job. If you can't think of another word, get your hands on a thesaurus.

Keeping things simple

Simple words are often short. They're words that your reader or listener understands, words they use in everyday language. For instance, terms like "size", "empty", and "stop" feel simpler than "magnitude", "unoccupied", and "discontinue". However, some words that appear long and complex may feel simple to some audiences. For instance, most seven-year-olds will feel completely comfortable with a term like "Tyrannosaurus Rex".

Simple words feel easy on the tongue. Words and phrases packed with consecutive consonants (like "setting down eight matchsticks lengthways") are difficult to pronounce and therefore difficult to read or hear. Blogger and branding consultant Christopher Johnson likens navigating phrases like this to city driving, complete with, "perilous lane changes and unexpected turns".[10]

Simple words are easy to follow. Terms that have different meanings in different contexts can easily catch people out. For instance, "vessel" means a boat or ship to some people and a cup or bowl to others. Words whose meanings are linked with their pronunciation cause particular trouble for readers. "Sewer", for instance, might mean a person who sews (pronounced *sow-er*) or a wastewater tunnel (pronounced *sue-er*). Listeners, on the other hand, may struggle with words that have the same pronunciation but different meanings, like "knight" and "night".

Being precise

When writers are advised to simplify their writing, they risk losing precision. They sometimes dumb a story down so much that they talk about "doing several things" rather than describing the reality (for instance, that someone is "holding down two jobs"). Or they'll say, in a vague tone, that someone spent their time "visiting places" rather than telling us that they "travelled to Rome, Paris, and Dubai".

Clarity shouldn't compromise specificity and meaning. Clarity comes from choosing the most appropriate understandable word (or words) to describe what you mean. For instance, words like "stare", "peer", and "glance" mean something far more specific in comparison with the term "look". "Strode", "stepped", and "ambled" offer more precision than "walked". And "tapped", "stroked", or "prodded" communicate far more than "touched".

If you struggle to find a single precise word that reflects reality, consider incorporating additional detail instead. A phrase like, "a rusty, lime-green camper van," tells us more than "a VW van", while "the dark, smoke-filled study" is more evocative than "the small room".

Though precision is important, beware being so precise that you distract from what matters. In particular, avoid any temptation to pack your dialogue with a thesaurus's worth of phrases like, "she proclaimed", "he declared", or "she uttered". When you read most professionally written dialogue, "she said" is the default format. Stick with that and your readers' and listeners' attention will fall on the spoken words not on how you opted to introduce them.

Writing to the format

You'll gain multiple benefits if you take time to consider your end format as you write. These include opportunities to:

- Tailor your writing to the shape and length of the available space.
- Craft a first line that fits within the constraints of social media.
- Visualise how your words will work alongside other media, like images and sounds.
- Use format constraints to improve the focus and style of your work.

When you draft copy in a program like MS Word it's easy to be duped into thinking your sentences and paragraphs are perfectly proportioned. But paste a chunk of text from Word into Twitter/X, Instagram, or a website and you'll gain a new perspective. Seeing your words on social media or on a mobile screen can transform a paragraph that felt short and to the point into an overwhelming wall of text.

As an example, a paragraph like the previous one takes up about five lines in Word, but 11 lines on Instagram. Reading it on my phone, it almost fills my entire screen. While comparisons like this vary across devices and settings, text that feels manageable while writing in Word may feel unmanageable when read or heard. One quick and easy way to keep the end format in mind is to set the line length in Word to mimic the line length of the platform or website where your story will be published.

How constraints improve your writing

The constraints built into some platforms may even improve your writing. For instance, when Electra Rhodes wrote her thread story, she never let a sentence run over into a new post. This forced Rhodes to "cut to the chase". With just 20 blocks of 280 characters at her disposal, her words had to be precise and concise, while still connecting with readers on an emotional level. As Rhodes puts it, this constraint stopped her from "flannelling around with lots of funny adjectives".[11]

Connecting with readers and listeners

Readers and listeners make two important connections when they read a non-fiction story.

1 A connection with the real people *in* a story.
2 A connection with the writer *of* the story.

The first connection is forged when readers and listeners find a person in the story – or the challenge they face – relatable. The second is prompted by the tone the writer uses and the language they employ.

Voice and tone

When we meet someone in real life, our feelings toward them are influenced, in part, by how they speak. The same goes for how people feel when they read or hear your writing. Your writing voice is the way you naturally write, a manifestation of your intrinsic personality and values – or, if you're writing for a client, a representation of the organisation's brand. However, just as we adjust how we speak when we talk to different types of people, our written voice changes depending on who we're writing for and what we're writing about.

We adopt a more serious tone if we're telling a story about a topic like structural racism and a lighter tone if we're recounting a tale about learning how to ride a unicycle. We might use an "innocent" tone, which relates the events of the story as if they are happening right now (with no knowledge of what's to come) or an "experienced" one, which draws on additional knowledge to interpret events.[12]

Inexperienced writers often write in an overly formal tone, using rarified vocabulary and tortuous sentence constructions. It's a habit fuelled by fear their writing won't be up to scratch. Bestselling horror writer Stephen King compares this "dressing up" of words to "dressing up a household pet in evening clothes", something that most people would be ashamed of. A far more effective approach is to be conversational – to write as you would speak. To paraphrase King: call taking a sh*t "taking a sh*t", not "an act of excretion".[13] As journalist Rosalind Coward says, Internet audiences are not looking for someone who talks down to them, but someone "who talks across to them as a friend", someone who is "personal, intimate, uninhibited, immediate and angry".[14]

Some people – and certainly some of my clients – view conversational writing as ungainly dumbing down, but even specialists and highly educated audiences appreciate clear, straightforward text, especially when they're reading or listening online – it helps them gather information and grasp what's going on as quickly and easily as possible. You might say it serves up the perfect, tasty meal to the hungry leopards we met in Chapter 1. We'll explore how to write as you would speak in more depth in Chapter 7.

Inclusive writing

Writers sometimes use devices like humour and metaphor to build a connection with their audience. Readers and listeners who "get" what's going on feel connected with the writer, as if they're in a special club. However, these devices may also exclude people; if someone doesn't get the point, they feel barred from the club. Aside from taking care with humour and metaphors, you can make readers and listeners feel more welcome by:

- Choosing words that everyone can understand. Or providing brief descriptions for readers and listeners who aren't in the know.
- Avoiding acronyms, Latin terms or specialist jargon – or defining and describing them.

- Assuming zero prior knowledge. Writing phrases like, "it's common knowledge" or "everyone knows" can put readers or listeners off too. What feels like common knowledge to you may not be to everyone else.

While these principles provide a useful starting point, truly inclusive writers acknowledge that language plays a role in perpetuating or challenging damaging societal structures. As Oxfam International cites in its *Inclusive Language Guide*, words may reinforce structures that, "maintain poverty, inequality and suffering". Even if you're not writing a political or awareness-raising story, it's worth reflecting on the words you use so you don't inadvertently reinforce damaging systems. That's why organisations like Oxfam have developed detailed guidelines that set out the language they aim to use and the terminology they want to move away from.

In practice: Oxfam's *Inclusive Language Guide*

Oxfam is part of a global charitable network that supports and mobilises people and communities to drive change. In 2022, 80 years after Oxfam was founded, CEO Dhananjayan Sriskandarajah announced that the organisation needed to re-imagine and remake itself. As part of this transformation, Oxfam wanted to make conscious choices about language. As its *Inclusive Language Guide* states, appropriate language may "reframe issues, rewrite tired stories, challenge problematic ideas and build a radically better future".

The *Guide* is a first step in an ongoing process, and one of many such guides produced by forward-thinking organisations. It includes over 150 preferred words selected in consultation with groups who advise on language preferred by marginalised people and communities. Key principles enshrined within the *Guide* include:

- Put people first. Emphasise the person, not the health condition or economic situation they live with.
- Give people agency. Appreciate that people survive or live with situations, instead of presenting them as passive victims.
- Avoid terms that perpetuate colonial, racist, or sexist attitudes, or that reinforce structural inequality.
- Avoid terms that patronise people or reinforce stereotypes.
- Respect the terms that communities choose to use themselves.
- Use terms that actively challenge structures that marginalise people.

Specific examples of some of the terms identified and explained within the *Guide* include:

- **Black** (not black). Black should be capitalised to align with how other ethnic identities (like Asian) are usually defined.

- **Transgender** (not transgendered or transsexual). This has a more positive connotation than words that have been used in the past.
- **Person living with AIDS** (not AIDS sufferer or AIDS victim). The person should not be defined by their health issue.
- **Survivor of rape** (not rape victim). This gives agency to the person who experienced rape.
- **Refugee** (not illegal migrant). A person can't be "illegal", though their actions may be.
- **Sex worker** (not prostitute). This is the term people who work in the sex industry use to describe themselves.
- **Global South** or **Global majority** (not developing or third-world countries). These terms shift understanding of global power and culture away from wealthier, white-majority nations.

These terms made sense for Oxfam when the *Guide* was published, but may not make sense for every organisation, or even for Oxfam in the future. Language is ever evolving, as is the world around us. What was appropriate or acceptable in the past may be inappropriate or damaging today. Guides like this will, as Oxfam itself acknowledges, need to be updated as societies change and justice movements develop.[15]

Oxfam's *Guide* is not intended as a strict rulebook – for the organisation or for others – but it does provide food for thought for all writers. Since writers choose and use words every day, why wouldn't we want to choose and use words that make the world a better place?

Dealing with exclusive language

If you've no option but to use language that may exclude some groups, look for ways to enable everyone to understand and enjoy the story. Perhaps you could incorporate definitions of specialist terms within the action? Or include an informative note about terminology somewhere, as the *Stolen Hearts* podcast does? Each episode of this show starts with an aside about the British vocabulary that listeners outside the UK may not understand. The announcement is delivered in a tone that matches the narration, so it doesn't sound too much like a language lesson. Here's the language note from episode 5.

For our American listeners, the following episode contains references to blanc-mange, which is a jelly-like dessert that is often bright pink in colour, and Welsh cakes, which are small, flat cakes with raisins and sugar, and objectively not as good as scones. This episode also contains some swearing.[16]

Like *Stolen Hearts*, some writers and publications also use content warnings to signal when a story includes topics or language (like swearing) that may upset or offend readers or listeners. Where there's a risk that material within a story might cause distress to people who have experienced traumatic events in the past, trigger warnings may also be useful. If you're not sure about the impact of your words, or the most appropriate language to use, seek advice from someone within the community you're writing about. Be humble in this regard. If you're not part of the community, you'll never know best.

Involving through storymaking

To a large extent, readers and listeners become involved in a story through its structure. They're drawn in by the challenge the person in the story faces and by a sequence of events that builds suspense. However, words play a role in focusing readers' and listeners' attention in a specific direction. They may also create opportunities for audiences to construct their own version of the story.

Giving readers and listeners space

To become involved in your writing, a reader or listener needs to build their own story from the events and information you share. They need space and time to do this. We'll explore how to create space within audio stories in Chapter 7. In text-based stories, line breaks between paragraphs are an easy way to create mental space. Images, subheadings, displayed quotes, or other design devices do a similar job.

In the example below, taken from the middle of Electra Rhodes's Twitter/X story, the space between consecutive posts enables Rhodes to step back from the action and comment on what's going on. Line spaces within the posts also play an important role.

> Tony and I did a spot of reconnaissance and schlepped between different sites in Wiltshire and Berks. Private land. Private land. Ancient monument. Shit. Pink's wife phoned. Maybe just an afternoon trip, pals? I think a night might be too much. Pink though? Such a stubborn git.

> What do you do when your friend says one thing, his wife says another, and you can hear death knocking at the outside door?
>
> I dunno about you.
>
> We went to Wayland's Smithy.

At the end of the first post we realise that Pink ("such a stubborn git") probably ignored his wife. But we're not sure. The next post opens with a question from Rhodes ("What do you do when ...?"). This, combined with another line space and a prompt for the reader to think about the issue ("I dunno about you"), holds our attention at what turns out to be a key pivot point in the story. The spaces in the story give *us* space to pause. We consider what we might do in similar circumstances, before discovering what Rhodes and Pink actually did ("We went to Wayland's Smithy").

Showing and telling

"Show don't tell" is one of the most commonly heard pieces of writing guidance. It's an instruction to *show* actions in preference to *telling* readers or listeners what's going on. One reason it's such a persistent piece of advice is that, as Ted Cheney says, readers and listeners, "don't like being told".[17] They believe what they see themselves over what they hear from someone else. Showing also fosters involvement by creating opportunities for readers and listeners to feel what people in the story feel.

As an example of showing vs telling, look at these two sentences.

> **Telling sentence**
>
> This would take place at the end of January – when temperatures are sometimes as low as minus 15 Celsius – at the 9,000-acre Tettegouche State Park in northern Minnesota.

> **Showing sentence**
>
> This would take place at the end of January – when temperatures sometimes drop so low your lungs might shatter if you take too deep a breath – at the 9,000-acre Tettegouche State Park in northern Minnesota.[18]

In the first example, we're *told* what temperatures in the Park might be. In the second, from Benjamin Percy's story about participating in a "Man Camp", we're *shown* the potential impact of such low temperatures. Percy's description helps us imagine how cold the Park might feel. It requires no prior knowledge about low temperatures and might even prompt us to gasp for breath.

An easy way to make sure that you're showing not telling is to avoid using verbs like "to be" or "to have", since they have no sense of action. Rather than writing "the door was closed" (where "was" simply describes the status of the door), try "the door blocked her path" (where "blocked" gives an impression that the door is doing something). In *Man Camp*, Percy does this when he says temperatures "drop" rather than temperatures "are". The key distinction here is that you want descriptions that are *active* ("the door blocks" or "temperatures drop") not *passive* ("the door was", "temperatures are").

Despite the ubiquity of "show don't tell", there are plenty of situations where telling is a useful writing strategy. After all, when we speak, we naturally tend to flip between showing and telling, so why not do the same in writing? Take this example from global consulting firm Korn Ferry's corporate website. The company's story begins in 1969.

> Korn Ferry started in a small office in Century City, Los Angeles; one phone, one assistant, and a coveted Rolodex of contacts. But the name on the door said everything: Korn/Ferry International – a vision of being global.[19]

Both sentences flip between showing and telling. We're told that Korn Ferry had a small office and then shown just how tiny. We're shown the company's full name at the time and then told what that signified. Telling serves a purpose here by delivering facts (like when the office was set up) and commentary (like the idea that the company's name reflected bold ambitions).

When to show

Showing is especially useful in the middle of your story, where there's a lot of action. It helps readers or listeners imagine themselves there in the moment, while leaving them to draw their own conclusions about what's going on. Showing can:

1 Focus the reader or listener's attention on action that drives the story forward. They'll infer more without you needing to spell everything out.
2 Help the reader or listener build visual images of what's going on. They'll live the story rather than have it told to them.
3 Prompt understanding about someone's personality or what they're feeling without needing to say something you couldn't possibly know. If you show the action, the reader or listener will draw their own conclusions about who that person is and how they might feel.

When to tell

Telling is especially useful at the start and end of your story, where you need to communicate key points quickly. It enables you to step out of the story and make clarifications or comments. Telling can:

1 Communicate a specific fact or point, leaving no room for misinterpretation.
2 Introduce abstract thoughts and generalisations, which help the reader or listener appreciate why the specific story you're telling matters.
3 Build tension by slowing down the pace of the action.

Using quotes and images

Quotes and images can show a facet of a scene, idea, or person too. In text-based stories, writers use them if they communicate an event or conjure up a location more effectively than their own words. In podcasts, quotes can play a far larger role, as we'll see in Chapter 7.

In the example below, from an online article on the website of London's Victoria & Albert Museum, a brief quote reveals more than the writer could. The piece tells the story of bestselling children's book *The Tale of Peter Rabbit,* written by Beatrix Potter. Published by Frederick Warne in 1902, the book sold unexpectedly well, as this paragraph explains.

> Within a year Warne was already planning a sixth printing. Potter was astonished: "The public must be fond of rabbits! What an appalling quantity of Peter".[20]

In just 13 words, this quote reveals an intriguing aspect of Potter's personality. Images play a similar role. They bring scenes to life and help readers slip into the world of the story. They reinforce the veracity of nonfiction, communicate nuanced concepts, and provide breaks in your prose. To see how this works in practice, let's consider how images were used within an online story I wrote about a teenage girl who contracted smallpox in 1896.[21] Published by Wellcome Collection, the story included three different types of images.

1 **Mood imagery.** A vivid archive illustration of a human arm and hand covered in glistening green pustules appears at the start of the story. This shows the reality of living with smallpox.
2 **Story imagery.** Photographs of the teenage girl (one taken in hospital, the other when she was convalescing) appear close to the beginning and end. They prompt readers to see the story from the girl's perspective, while reinforcing that this happened to a real person.
3 **Content imagery.** A handful of archive cartoons illustrating a common contemporary fear about vaccination appear in the middle of the story. While the content point is explained in the text, the cartoons do a far better job communicating the depth of public feeling.

Balancing events and details

Events move the story forward. Details help us picture the events and understand what's going on. Advertising strategist Martin Weigel describes events as "movement" and detail as "colour". For Weigel, "movement without colour fails to elaborate what we mean. Colour without movement is a useless tone poem."[22] Stories need a mix of both. Pack your story full of too many events and it's difficult to understand what is happening. Cram in too much detail and you reduce your story to a stream of consciousness.

Let's look at how these two elements balance out in the origin story of soft drinks business Aunty's Ginger Tonic. The story told on the brand's website begins with an *event-focused* sentence, which moves the action forward.

> Yarrie's memories of her African heritage inspired her to start making the special ginger brew that she drank in her youth.

Later, we have a *detail-focused* paragraph, which provides context about the founder's values.

> To Yarrie, Aunty's Ginger Tonic isn't a business. It's a symbol of her past, her future and the power of community.[23]

Without the first sentence, we'd have no idea how the business started. Without the later ones, the brand would fail to communicate its core reason for being.

Transporting readers and listeners into the story

Readers and listeners become transported into a story when they visualise what's happening and the story feels real. Writers achieve this through clever use of pace, tense, and sensory information. They also take conscious steps to keep readers and listeners *in* the story.

Pace

Writing a story isn't like writing a detailed timeline of events. Nonfiction writers don't cover everything that ever happened. Nor do they allot the same number of words to each period of time within the story. They may dwell at some points and gloss over others. Sometimes they want readers or listeners to float along gently. Sometimes they rush them through treacherous rapids.

Changes in pace focus readers' or listeners' attention on specific moments. For instance, if you draw out an experience that lasted a matter of seconds in real life, we'll realise it's an important moment in the story. The ideal is to rush through the boring (but necessary) parts of the story. Then slow down and stretch out time in the vital moments. It's like filming in slow-motion. Keep sentences short. Focus on action not description. Pause. Insert a line break.

Maybe pose a question? Pause again. Overall, aim to expand a brief moment into several lines, as this description of a broken laptop does.

> It wouldn't turn on. We pressed the button … we held it down … we punched it. We prayed. We rocked the computer back and forth … caressed it tenderly … then gave it a whack and made sure it was fully charged … [24]

Repetition also focuses readers' or listeners' attention onto specific moments or issues. For instance, in a story about living with Hepatitis C, author Ijeoma Oluo uses the same phrase three times.

> For almost two decades I lived like my blood was a ticking timebomb. For almost two decades I had to warn every partner, every doctor, every dentist to stay away from my blood. For almost two decades every sore muscle was a sign that it was getting worse, every forgotten task was a sign the brain fog was setting in.[25]

By repeating "for almost two decades", Oluo draws attention to the sheer length of time she was forced to endure these challenges.

Tense

Glance back at the extracts used throughout this chapter and you'll see most are written in the past tense. This shouldn't be a surprise, given they describe events that took place *in the past*. The past tense is a common and appropriate approach when talking about real events. This is particularly true if you use the past present (e.g. "she bought" or "he ran"), which feels punchier than the past imperfect (e.g. "she was buying" or "he was running").

However, the present tense can transport readers and listeners into a moment far more effectively. Take this example from a story by Augusta Declan about posing for social media shots.

> She tells me to smile, then to stop smiling. To move my hands, and then to remove them from under my chin. It's too old-fashioned, too boring. She says to point my toes, to stop standing akimbo, to stop scowling so fiercely.
> *"Hike up your dress. Play with the flowers. Stop slouching! Suck your belly in."*
> She's getting frustrated, and I am too.[26]

Declan's writing is direct and active. We feel like we're there, even that we're Declan herself. Personally, I couldn't help straightening my back and pulling my belly in … The same information presented in the past tense wouldn't deliver the same impact.

Because tense signals when things happen (or happened), a change in tense can distinguish between events in the story and broader commentary. For example, in the *Man Camp* article we met earlier, this sentence uses two tenses.

> This was the sort of thing I feared when signing up for Man Camp, the thing so many men fear.

The first half of the sentence uses the past tense. It tells us what happened (the writer *was* scared). The second half of the sentence uses the present tense. It links that specific event to what happens in the wider world (men *are* scared).

Drawing on all the senses

So far, I've emphasised the importance of visual details, since they help readers and listeners picture your story. However, details that draw on all the senses can transport readers and listeners into a key moment too. Take a look at this extract from a *National Geographic* blog written by Douglas Fox, which describes an encounter with humpback whales.

> The water erupts just ahead of our boat – a blow of mist. It hovers, drifts in the breeze, dampens our faces, jackets, and hands. My notebook is coated in dew. Then we smell it.
>
> The odor is blunt and pungent, almost a taste in the mouth, an unholy mingling of fart and fishiness – hundreds of gallons of air forcefully expelled from its lungs, laced with the fumes of half-digested krill, hundreds of pounds of these slow-dissolving crustaceans fermenting in its stomach.[27]

In this extract, we *see* the water blowing in the air ahead of the boat, like mist. We *feel* that mist fall on the skin of our face and hands. We *smell* farts and fish. We *taste* the disgusting flavour of fermenting shellfish.

Sensory details prompt neurological responses that mimic what happens in our brains when we feel these experiences for real. For instance, when you read a word that describes a smell (like turpentine, garlic, poo, jasmine, or cinnamon), the brain areas sparked when your nose picks up a smell become active. When you read a word that describes a texture (like leathery or rough), texture-related brain areas become active. Reading a smelly or touchy word in your head, then, prompts a similar response to smelling or touching the real thing.[28]

Staying in the story

Readers or listeners may be distracted away from a story for all sorts of reasons. Ideally none should come from the story itself. If your audience has become involved in the story, they want to stick around. To keep them with you, avoid doing anything that might jolt them out of the moment. Use language and phrasing that's appropriate to the events and the historical setting. Maintain a consistent tone and tense. When things change, ease people from one place or time to another. And don't give any reason for anyone to doubt the facts of the matter.

Ensuring smooth transitions

When sequential events in your story take place in different locations or at different times you must transition between them. Gary Provost calls transitions "danger zones" because they're the moments in a story when you're at greatest risk of losing your reader or listener. To guide readers and listeners through the danger, build a bridge between what they've just read or heard and what comes next. Aside from communicating what's happening, try using what Provost calls "bridge words", words or phrases that appear in both sentences, like echoes bouncing across a ravine.[29]

Sometimes a single word or phrase is enough to span the ravine (see what I did there?). Familiar terms like "later", "the following day", "back at base", or "at the other end of the street" often do the job perfectly well. Sometimes, however, you need one or more lines of telling to bind scenes together. This is especially true if you leap across long periods of time. For example, in a Black History Month story about NASA mathematician Katherine Johnson, a single telling sentence acts as a bridge between the work Johnson completed for NASA in the late 1950s and her contribution to the Moon landing a decade later.

Then, in 1962, President John F. Kennedy charged the country to send a man to the moon.[30]

Armed with this fact, we're primed for the next line, which begins "Johnson became part of the team, and she began to work on calculating the trajectory for America's first space trip ..."

Dealing with uncertainty

Readers and listeners need to feel confident that you've done your research and that the story you're telling is accurate and complete. Sadly, there will always be information that you haven't been able to source. To fill in the gaps you may need to speculate. If so, you *must* flag that this material is not undisputed fact.

If writing in the first person you might use phrases like, "I imagine", "it seemed to me", or "I suppose". In the third person, essayist Lisa Knopp recommends what she calls "perhapsing", where the word "perhaps" signals to the reader or listener that what comes next is speculation. [31] This approach is used in the opening episode of the *Death of an Artist* podcast, when curator Helen Molesworth speculates about the attraction evident between artists Carl Andre and Ana Mendieta on the night they first meet.

> Carl paid Ana a lot of attention. Perhaps his left-wing politics led him to be interested in an exile from Cuba. Perhaps he could sense an affinity between their art – both were exploring the horizontal quality of the floor, the ground and the earth as a space for sculpture. Perhaps it was just your typical heterosexual shenanigans, as Ana was undeniably charismatic and attractive, and Carl had the shine of artworld fame and stardom. [32]

Prompting action through closing lines

Writing coach Jack Hart says of final lines: "a good one will sum up, surprise a little, perhaps bring things full circle". [33] The first job of any story end is to show how the story challenge was resolved. If we return to Brooke Chang's story about lying awake, her head abuzz with thought after thought, we discover:

> It's now 4:53am, and it seems like the demons in my head have quieted down. Maybe I can sneak in a few more hours of sleep.

Chang's first sentence resolves the challenge. The second poses a new question: will Chang manage to finally get some sleep? Though final lines may linger afterwards like this, writers shouldn't. Don't stick around at the end like an unwanted party guest.

Telling can be a useful approach to employ at this final stage. For instance, if we revisit Madhuraa Prakash's story about her experience of casual racism, the final lines feature a lot of telling.

> There's a big community of people in Australia who are culturally diverse, and we're all working together to fight the same battle. You are truly not alone in whatever you're feeling. There will always be a place for you to feel included and accepted.

If Prakash's readers visit ReachOut's website because they, or someone they know, struggle with issues like cultural identity and racism, the closing links provide clear guidance on what to do next. Readers are given options to consult tips on dealing with racism, read a story about how another young person connected with her cultural identity, or explore a collection of stories and advice about cultural identity.

Sometimes, endings are open and thought-provoking, like the closing line from the Art Institute of Chicago story about anonymous makers.

> I pictured a German man with calloused hands, maybe sitting at a table after a hard day's work, holding a small chisel and carving his name on a wooden heart with careful movements, hoping that someday, someone somewhere might see it and think of him. Whoever he might've been.

Quotes make for particularly striking endings. In a story about animator Steve Williams, who busted expectations by creating convincing computer-generated dinosaurs for the first *Jurassic Park* film, communication and creativity consultant Beth Collier ends with Williams's own words:

> "I love the term 'You will never'", Williams said. "If I listened to the people who said, 'You will never … ', T-Rex wouldn't have been built."[34]

This inspirational moment may prompt a reader to think differently in the future. A little further down the page, Collier builds on this by issuing a clear call to action, which links Williams's story to her own professional consultancy.

> If you know someone who needs help coming up with better ideas, and wants to build a culture where creativity and innovation thrive, please tell them to <u>get in touch</u>.

Though closing lines mark the end of a story for your reader or listener, the closing line in your first draft is unlikely to be the end for you. First drafts are rarely publication-ready. Before you move on, save your work. Close the file. Don't open it again. Wait at least a day – ideally longer. When you come back to it, your mind will have mulled everything over. Your eyes will see everything anew. Only then will you be ready to revise, edit, and publish your story, tasks that we'll cover in Chapter 8.

Summary

- Your writing voice is a consistent manifestation of your intrinsic personality and values (or those of your client). Your tone may vary depending on who you're writing for and what you're writing about.
- Humour and metaphor can build intimacy with audiences. To some readers and listeners they might, however, feel exclusive.
- Language plays a role in perpetuating or challenging societal structures that maintain poverty, inequality, and suffering.
- Showing is a useful approach in the middle of your story; telling plays an important role at the start and end.
- Sensory details transport readers or listeners into a story.
- Opening lines gain attention by introducing a person who does something, or an idea or issue. Surprising or provocative lines work particularly well.
- Closing lines sum up and surprise. While readers or listeners may take action without prompting, some include explicit calls to action.

Practical lessons for online writers

- **Aim for clarity above all else.** Get your thinking straight first. Then describe events in the order in which they happened.
- **Introduce new ideas slowly.** Limit each sentence to just one idea. Aim to keep sentences below 25 words.
- **Use simple, meaningful words.** Choose words that are familiar, specific, and precise, and which don't exclude anyone.
- **Treat words like a scarce commodity.** Don't dump extra information or unnecessary words in your story. Only include what advances the story, and what your reader or listener needs in that moment.
- **Give readers space.** Build in strategic line breaks so readers have a moment to absorb or reflect on what they've just read.
- **Stay in the moment.** Maintain a consistent point of view, tone, and tense. If any of these change, create smooth transitions that keep readers or listeners in the story.
- **Adopt inclusive language.** Be aware of the impact of your word choices. Consult inclusive language guides if need be, or talk to people within the communities you're writing about.
- **Be honest about speculation.** Make it clear that you are inventing (or "perhapsing") what might have happened.

Recommended reading

Jack Hart, *The Complete Guide to Writing Narrative Nonfiction* (Chicago: The University of Chicago Press, 2011) – comprehensive guide to all aspects of writing nonfiction stories. Chapter 7: "Action" provides particularly useful guidance for writers.

Joseph M Williams, *Style: Ten Lessons in Clarity and Grace* (Reading, MA: Addison-Wesley, 1997) – highly practical guide to the principles of writing, which feels like an intensive bootcamp for writers at any level.

Notes and references

1   Gary Provost, *100 Ways to Improve Your Writing* (New York: 1985)
2   <https://medium.com/bouncin-and-behavin-blogs/maybe-unemployment-is-a-blessing-in-disguise-7531f35a4b29> (accessed 2 August 2023)
3   <https://au.reachout.com/articles/madhuraas-story-you-dont-belong-here> (accessed 2 August 2023)
4   <https://wellcomecollection.org/articles/XIY2IRAAAHtGO1jP> Licensed under a CC BY 4.0 international licence: <https://creativecommons.org/licenses/by/4.0/> (both accessed 2 August 2023)
5   <https://www.artic.edu/articles/625/whittling-away-in-anonymity> (accessed 2 August 2023)
6   William Zinsser, *On Writing Well: The Classic Guide to Writing Nonfiction* (New York: Harper Perennial, 2016)
7   <https://twitter.com/electra_rhodes/status/1618246238742224904> (accessed 2 August 2023)
8   Roy Peter Clark, *How to Write Short: Word Craft for Fast Times* (New York: Little, Brown, 2013)
9   William Zinsser, *On Writing Well: The Classic Guide to Writing Nonfiction* (New York: Harper Perennial, 2016)
10 Christopher Johnson, *Microstyle: The Art of Writing Little* (New York: WW Norton, 2011)
11 Personal conversation with Electra Rhodes, 22 February 2023
12 The idea of innocent and experienced tones comes from Sue William Silverman in Sherry Ellis, *Now Write! Nonfiction: Memoir, Journalism, and Creative Nonfiction Exercises from Today's Best Writers and Teachers* (New York: Jeremy P Tarcher / Penguin, 2009)
13 Stephen King, *On Writing: A Memoir of the Craft* (London: Hodder, 2012)
14 Rosalind Coward, *Speaking Personally: The Rise of Subjective and Confessional Journalism* (Basingstoke: Palgrave Macmillan, 2013)
15 Oxfam International, *Inclusive Language Guide* (Oxford: Oxfam GB, 2023) <https://doi.org/10.21201/2021.7611> (extracts reproduced with the permission of Oxfam, www.oxfam.org.uk. Oxfam does not necessarily endorse any text or activities that accompany the materials); Dhananjayan Sriskandarajah, "As Oxfam Turns 80, Here are Three Big Ideas that I Think Will Shape its Future", Oxfam, 19 October 2022 <https://views-voices.oxfam.org.uk/2022/10/as-oxfam-turns-80-here-are-three-big-ideas-that-i-think-will-shape-its-future/>; Helen Wishart, "Words Matter", Oxfam, 13 March 2023 <https://views-voices.oxfam.org.uk/2022/10/as-oxfam-turns-80-here-are-three-big-ideas-that-i-think-will-shape-its-future/> (all accessed 7 June 2023)
16 Wondery, "A Crock of Sh*t", *Stolen Hearts*, podcast, 27 February 2023 <https://wondery.com/shows/stolen-hearts/episode/12149-a-crock-of-sht/> (accessed 8 June 2023)

17 Theodore A Rees Cheney, *Writing Creative Nonfiction: How to Use Fiction Techniques to Make Your Nonfiction More Interesting, Dramatic, and Vivid* (Berkeley, CA: Ten Speed Press, 1987)

18 <https://www.guernicamag.com/benjamin-percy-man-camp/> (accessed 2 August 2023) "Man Camp" ©2015 by Benjamin Percy. Originally published by *Guernica*. Used by permission Curtis Brown Ltd.

19 <https://www.kornferry.com/about-us/our-story> (accessed 2 August 2023)

20 <https://www.vam.ac.uk/articles/peter-rabbit-the-tale-of-the-tale> (accessed 2 August 2023) ©Victoria and Albert Museum London

21 <https://wellcomecollection.org/articles/WsT4Ex8AAHruGfXd> (accessed 2 August 2023)

22 Martin Weigel, *Strategy Needs Good Words*, Martin Weigel, 20 March 2019 <https://www.martinweigel.org/mrweigelgmailcom/2019/03/20/strategy-needs-good-words> (accessed 3 April 2023)

23 <https://www.auntysgingertonic.com.au/our-story> (accessed 2 August 2023) Copy from Yarrie Bangura and her website for her business Aunty's Ginger Tonic. All rights reserved.

24 <https://bonnerprivateresearch.substack.com/p/under-attack> (accessed 2 August 2023)

25 <https://medium.com/@IjeomaOluo/your-body-just-wants-to-get-through-this-229be0217b4e> (accessed 23 April 2023)

26 <https://kalaharireview.com/posing-for-the-camera-3c94e09552c6> (accessed 2 August 2023)

27 <https://www.nationalgeographic.com/adventure/article/this-is-what-whale-breath-smells-like> (accessed 2 August 2023) Copyright Douglas Fox, originally published 19 April 2016 on nationalgeographic.com

28 Julio Gonzalez et al., "Reading Cinnamon Activates Olfactory Brain Regions", *NeuroImage*, 32 (2006), 906–12 <https://doi.org/10.1016/j.neuroimage.2006.03.037>; Simon Lacey et al., "Metaphorically Feeling: Comprehending Textual Metaphors Activates Somatosensory Cortex", *Brain and Language*, 120: 3 (2012) 416–21 <https://doi.org/10.1016/j.bandl.2011.12.016>

29 Gary Provost, *100 Ways to Improve Your Writing*

30 <https://www.blackhistorymonth.org.uk/article/section/science-and-medicine/katherine-johnson-a-lifetime-of-stem/> (accessed 2 August 2023)

31 Lisa Knopp, "Perhapsing", in *Now Write! Nonfiction: Memoir, Journalism, and Creative Nonfiction Exercises from Today's Best Writers and Teachers*, ed. Sherry Ellis (New York: Jeremy P Tarcher / Penguin, 2009), pp. 61–3

32 Helen Molesworth, "The Haunting, Death of an Artist", podcast, Pushkin, September 2022 <https://www.pushkin.fm/podcasts/death-of-an-artist/episode-1-the-haunting> (accessed 8 June 2023)

33 Jack Hart, *The Complete Guide to Writing Narrative Nonfiction* (Chicago: University of Chicago Press, 2011)

34 <https://bethcollier.substack.com/p/how-one-maverick-changed-jurassic> (accessed 2 August 2023) Curious Minds, by Beth Collier

7 Writing for listeners

This chapter considers the specific context of writing nonfiction stories that will be listened to. It incorporates examples from a variety of successful podcasts, while drawing on the expertise of writers working in radio. The chapter covers:

- How writing for listeners differs from writing for readers
- Writing as you would speak
- Keeping listeners' interest
- Signposting what's happening
- Working with pre-recorded content
- Presenting an audio script

Before I discovered podcasts, I never really got audio. I liked the idea of listening on the go, but most audiobooks failed to hold my attention. If I listened to a novel or an authoritative biography, I felt as if I was being lectured to. Only when I turned to memoirs presented in a direct, conversational style did I finally feel any connection with audio stories and their writers.

I struggle with most audiobooks because they do just about everything you *shouldn't* do when writing for audio. Though there are exceptions (notably among audio-first publications), many audiobooks feel complex and challenging. Narrated in a formal, actorly voice, with limited signposting and murky transitions, they're hard to follow and easy to lose interest in.

These problems arise because an audiobook is usually an adaptation of a book written *to be read*. Podcasts, on the other hand, grew out of radio: a medium that attracts, entertains and involves *listeners*.

Podcasts are a treasure trove of engaging nonfiction writing. They provide templates, not just for aspiring audio storytellers, but for anyone who wants to write stories that connect with readers and listeners. This chapter identifies what makes audio special, before sharing best practice in writing stories that will be listened to. It highlights the value of recorded interviews

DOI: 10.4324/9781003363347-9

(known as "tape") and explores how to guide your listener through a story at a pace that works for them.

What makes audio special?

In many ways writing for an online listener demands a similar approach to writing for an online reader. Listeners and online readers all benefit from being thrown straight into the action. They appreciate succinct, focused stories, and feel connected with writers who adopt an informal, conversational tone. There are, however, a number of aspects that set writing for audio apart.

- **Greater expectation of connection.** Listeners expect to feel connected with whoever is telling the story, as if they're hearing it directly from a friend.
- **Possible distractions.** Radio and spoken-word writer Jules Horne describes her listener as, "a distracted, slightly deaf reveller in a noisy pub".[1] These revellers struggle to catch every word and easily lose track of what's happening.
- **Lack of visual cues.** Listeners aren't able to use visual hints to help them navigate the story. They have no headings, paragraph breaks, or other visual design elements to indicate when sections start or finish.
- **Imposed listening speed.** While listeners may pause or rewind an audio file if necessary, audio stories move on at the pace of the narrator, not the pace of the listener. Listeners have little time to decode complex ideas or unravel convoluted sentences. It's not easy to glance back at an earlier paragraph or skip forward to see what's coming.
- **An evolving script.** The written script isn't the final product. It will be interpreted and performed to create the final story. The narrator (even if they are the writer) affects the pace, tone, and emphasis of the words that the listener hears.

If you're writing for audio, you'll need to write as you would speak and take extra care to help readers understand where they are in the story. You must guide readers through everything, step by step, giving an explicit signal when something important is shared. You should signpost every moment when you change time, location, or perspective.

Writing for a listener

When you write for audio, your aim should be to produce what storytelling coach Kevin Anderson and podcaster Colin Gray call an "invisible script".[2] While the best storytelling podcasts are meticulously scripted, their narration sounds spontaneous, like a natural, human conversation. Although writing in such an informal tone doesn't come easily to everyone, there are a few rules of thumb that can keep you on the right track. The first is to write in a conversational style.

If I asked you to explain your course or your job to a colleague in an email, what would you write? Now, what if I asked you to explain it to them in person? Do your two responses match? Usually, our written and spoken language differ. When we speak, we arrange words and phrases in more straightforward structures. We tend to use simpler words, introduce ideas sequentially, and speak in an active tone.

A conversational style should sound authentic and familiar. Don't try to impress. Instead, use contractions, introduce pauses, and rely on words recognisable to your listener. Talk about "I" and "you". Include the odd one-word interjection ("yay", "d'oh", or "phew"). And break some traditional grammar rules – whether that's by starting sentences with "and", "but", and "or" or by writing in fragmented prose.

When we speak in real life we stumble, hesitate, repeat ourselves, and use unnecessary words. So, when I say, "write in a conversational style", the word *style* is key. Many real-life conversations are dull, rambling monologues that no one would ever choose to listen to. Audio stories should be written with the voice and tone of everyday conversation, without reproducing the chaotic inanity of real speech.

Simple words

The easiest way to write as you would speak is to speak before you write. Tell the story out loud, as if you were telling it to someone else, and then write down what you say – or record yourself and transcribe the recording. When you do this, you'll naturally find yourself using simple, no-nonsense language. Simple in this context doesn't just mean short and uncomplicated – like saying "so" and "also" instead of "consequently" and "furthermore". Simple words should also be easy to pronounce. To see what I mean, try saying the following phrase out loud: "If you use statistical data, you'll present an authoritative image". It's a sentence I recently found myself saying in an audio recording for professionals. While it's not particularly complex, it *is* difficult to say without stumbling. So, stick with words that won't interrupt the flow of the narrator, even if the narrator is you.

Simple should never mean bland. Vary your vocabulary, choose striking words when needed, and make the most of audio by writing with sound and rhythm in mind. Consider addressing the listener directly too. Saying "you" is one of the easiest ways to build a connection with your listener, an approach we don't often apply in other writing formats.

Active language

When we speak, we use active language, which is easier to follow and more dynamic than many types of writing. To see what I mean, read these two statements out loud and listen to yourself. Which feels more natural?

> **Statement 1**
>
> Wendy ate her breakfast at 10am.

> **Statement 2**
>
> Breakfast was eaten by Wendy at 10am.

The first statement sounds closest to how most people usually speak. Statement 2 sounds more like a statement from an official report. This is because Statement 1 is an *active* sentence, while Statement 2 is a *passive* one.

We describe sentences as active when the subject of the sentence is a person (in this case, Wendy) who takes action and does something (in this case, eating her breakfast). The second statement is passive because the subject is the breakfast, which doesn't do anything (it is simply eaten by Wendy). The word "was" is a bit of a giveaway in Statement 2, a clue that can help you spot other passive phrases in your writing. Try searching for "was" in your script and you might find other phrases that could be rearranged into an active form.

Being you

If you're writing a script that you will be recording, the script should – of course – sound like you. This means using words that you would say in every-day speech, while revealing something of your personality. For radio journalist David Greene, showing your personality comes from letting listeners hear, "how you're reacting to what you learn, let them hear your wit, let them hear when something makes you sad or strikes you as odd".[3]

A useful tip for writing like "you" is to write, say Kevin Anderson and Colin Gray, "with your filters off".[4] Include anecdotes, jokes, or quips when they come to you – anything that reflects the natural way you speak. Put all this material in your first draft so you have something to work with. When you come to edit your story, switch your filters back on and decide what to keep and what to edit out.

Opening your audio story

When listeners start an audio story, it's not easy to skip forward. The intro-duction therefore needs to work hard to retain people's attention. This is markedly different to the beginning of text stories, where readers might skip over introductory material in order to get to the heart of the story as quickly as possible.

Effective audio beginnings make the story's focus clear, give an idea of what to expect, and generate momentum, all in a matter of seconds. They should also help listeners attune to the voice of the narrator.

If you're unclear where to start, NPR editorial specialist Alison MacAdam advises sticking with what grabbed *you*.[5] If there's a fact or question that sparked your interest, or a moment of tape that stopped you in your tracks, chances are it will do the same for your listeners. Some of the most common ways to open up a podcast are to:

- Pose a question, which gets the listener thinking about an issue.
- Introduce a mystery, which the host then attempts to solve.
- Outline a big idea, which identifies the angle of the story.
- Describe a physical location or a key story moment, which acts like a cinematic scene-setter.
- Meet the host, so listeners connect to the person/people who will guide them through the story.

Let's look at examples of each of these podcast openers now.

Pose a question

In the "Maidens' Voyage" episode of the Migration Museum's *Departures* podcast, host Mukti Jain Campion starts by posing two questions.

> How far would you travel to find love?
> Can you imagine crossing the ocean to marry a total stranger?[6]

These questions set the scene for an episode about emigration from England in the early 1600s. It's a story of young women being shipped across the Atlantic Ocean to help establish a new English colony in Jamestown, Virginia.

The first of these two questions might lead to any number of stories. If used on its own, it leaves a gaping chasm between the attention-grabber and the actual story. The second question narrows the focus, drawing listeners closer to what follows. If used without the first question, listeners might, however, struggle to leap straight into a story that's probably far from their own experience. By using both questions, listeners are guided from a universal issue (finding love) to a specific tale (marrying a total stranger in a faraway land).

Introduce a mystery

In some question openings, the narrator highlights a mystery they will then attempt to solve. This approach is commonly heard in true-crime shows, where the host plays the role of investigator. If you're attempting to solve a mystery in your audio story, pose a question (or two) at the start, as I did in the first episode of *Bookshapers*:

> For most people, writing a book is a big challenge, even more so if you then publish it. But what if you're doing all that in a cramped and stinky, flat-pack hut? In the darkest, most inhospitable place on Earth?[7]

The episode goes on to explore how explorers in 1907 wrote, illustrated, and printed the first book ever published in Antarctica.

Outline a big idea

The "Refusing to Feed" episode of the *Bodies* podcast tells a story about a woman's struggle to get her new-born baby to feed. The episode starts with host Allison Behringer saying:

> Having a baby must be incredible. It must also be terrifying. You have to care for every detail – details that can mean life or death. You have this immense responsibility to do the best thing. But there are so many ways to be a parent! How do you know what's best? One thing that does seem clear to me: no matter how much you prepare, no matter how much you know, motherhood is often nothing like what you expect.[8]

This opener gives little hint about the specific nature of the story we're about to hear. Instead, it highlights the angle the story takes: that it's never easy for parents to know the best thing to do. This big idea resonates as we listen on, guiding us to view the story through that specific lens.

Describe a key story moment

Episode 2 of the *Stolen Hearts* podcast opens with this description.

> Her Majesty's Prison Elmley is a warren of ugly yellow-brick buildings – like a network of warehouses contained within a formidable concrete wall. Inside the housing blocks, it looks like every gritty British prison drama you've ever seen: three floors of beige walls, steel railings and a net to stop anyone from jumping. And row after row of prison cells: narrow rooms with a toilet and a mattress. In one cell is prisoner VH4265, Dean Jenkins.[9]

When I first listened to this, I felt like I was watching one of the gritty prison dramas it references. I visualised the camera sweeping across a wide shot of the ugly yellow buildings, drawing closer and closer, before zooming into a single cell. The episode then tells the story of how Jenkins ended up there.

A similar example comes from *Shame in Medicine*, a podcast produced by a community of healthcare workers known as The Nocturnists. Episode 7 begins with a scene described by the main person in the story, Dr Gita Pensa. "So, my attorney – every day before court, and on the first day, especially", begins Pensa, "I had to meet him at his office. And he was like, 'I'm going to drive you to the courthouse'. And it was interesting because he drove me in a pickup truck."[10] Pensa goes on to explain what happened on that first day, from arriving at the courtroom and passing through the metal detector to listening to the judge. We learn what Pensa heard and how she felt. Her description ends with these five sentences.

> Nothing makes sense. You don't even know who to trust. You don't know what to believe. You don't know if your skillset is going to help you in any way. You have no idea what the heck is happening.

Coming from the person who experienced this moment, an introduction like this encourages us to put ourselves in their shoes. We picture the scene, empathise with how Pensa felt, and become anxious about what might happen next. The episode then goes on to tell the story of how Pensa ended up on trial.

Meet the host

Radio script editor Bill Ash recommends beginning with a likeable, identifiable individual – the person who ends up being your listener's guide.[11] This might be your narrator, or one of the key people interviewed for the story. If listeners don't connect with this person, they'll soon switch off.

One episode of the *Stuff you Missed in History Class* podcast starts with host Holly Frey confiding to co-host Tracy V Wilson that she's, "using the podcast for personal therapy". In the lively conversation that follows, Frey says she really doesn't like the word "kissing". It grosses her out, though she has no idea why. Frey uses any other word she can, even if it sounds silly. She jokes that she needs to deal with this issue. This is why, Frey says, she and Wilson are going to talk about kissing, "all day today". It's an entertaining way to get to know the pair, while also:

- **Getting our attention.** We're intrigued. We wonder what Frey's problem with the word kissing has got to do with the story.
- **Getting us thinking.** We're pulled into an aspect of the story (even though we don't yet know what that story is). We think about kissing, how we feel about it and how we feel talking about it.

We soon discover that this episode is about a woman who tried to get people to stop kissing – that's an intriguing hook in itself. But, says Frey, "there's more to this". She tells us that the story will include "communicable diseases" and "people being resistant" – both topics people felt strongly about when the episode aired (during the Covid-19 pandemic). This additional information highlights why the story matters. We connect it with our experience and current concerns, even though the events took place over 100 years ago. And all that's achieved in just one minute of preliminary chit-chat.

Whichever type of opener you use, your next job is to keep people listening. You'll succeed if you're realistic about the level of information a listener can absorb and make a conscious effort to hold their attention. Let's look at each of these writing challenges in turn.

Sharing the right information at the right time

Have you ever explained something to someone in precise detail, only to watch their eyes glaze over? Chances are, you covered too much ground too quickly and they simply lost interest. This is more likely to be a problem for listeners than readers, since readers are able to pause, re-read, and think through what they're reading. Listeners don't have the same opportunities unless you create them for them. Whatever information *you* think is important, it's vital to consider your listener and how much *they* can cope with. Radio scriptwriter Annie Caulfield puts it this way: "the trick is to think more about holding the listener's interest than getting the information across".[12] Slowing the pace, introducing new ideas one by one, recapping information, and using visual descriptions all play a role here.

Pace

In general, audio stories unfold at a slower pace than stories written to be read. To get the pace right, Caulfield recommends making notes of how little information the listener needs in order to understand what's happening. It's a tactic I've learned from teaching. It's no good turning up in a lecture hall with a long list of information you want to pump into students' brains. If you focus solely on what you want to communicate, you end up racing through everything in order to fit it in. Students can't keep up and you may as well have said nothing. If I work through the essential points at a pace that students feel comfortable with – and resist the temptation to cram in more – students listen and stay involved.

Journalist and podcaster Marc Fennell likens this drip feeding of information to how people write thrillers. You can, he says, "give people enough information to build a certain kind of image in their head. Then you can gradually give them more, gradually give them more, gradually give them more."[13]

Introducing new ideas

Good practice for any online writing is to keep sentences under 25 words. In an audio context, it's even more important to stay short and focused. From the narrator's point of view, it can be tough to get through a 40-word sentence without pausing for breath. From the listeners' side, long, rambling sentences are difficult to follow. So keep things short and introduce one idea per phrase or sentence.

The most problematic sentences are those that nest facts or ideas within other information. In grammar terms, these sentences include "subordinate" or "dependent" clauses. In the example below, these clauses are separated from the main content by commas and dashes:

> Anna Faherty, whose first ever story featured a small cuddly panda, spoke to us about the everyday struggles she faces – as a busy freelance writer, and a part-time lecturer – now.

Alison MacAdam labels sentences like this, "toxic". MacAdam's antidote is to rearrange the words so the subjects of your sentences get "cosy with their verbs".[14] In this example, the subject is "Anna Faherty" (me), but there are nine words before the verb that tells us I spoke. Not very cosy at all.

You can identify toxic sentences by looking out for multiple commas, dashes, or ands. Plentiful punctuation marks are usually a symptom that you're covering too many ideas. Break-up a toxic sentence each time you hit a punctuation mark and you'll create shorter sentences, each focusing on just one fact or idea, like this:

> Anna Faherty's first ever story featured a small cuddly panda. Now she's a freelance writer and a part-time lecturer. Anna spoke to us about the everyday struggles she faces while writing.

In reality, we don't always speak in full sentences, though. We may pause, refocus and jump to something new, with little regard for the established rules of grammar. Conversational sentence structure is therefore more fluid than we usually accept in writing. In audio, punctuation is less important (because the listener doesn't use it to navigate through our words) and fragmented sentences are perfectly acceptable. Take this extract, for example, which comes from an episode of the *Family Secrets* podcast narrated by Dani Shapiro:

> One of the things I've noticed about family secrets [...] is that often, if somebody is, say, a writer, an artist, a playwright, a film-maker, she or he ends up with a very strong impulse to tell the story, to make something out of it, to turn all that weird silence, shame, confusion and betrayal into a narrative – into something that shines a bright light into the darkness.[15]

While this fragmented sentence includes more than 25 words, Shapiro's approach is far more suited to audio then the rambling sentence I used as an example above. Shapiro's writing works because she sticks with the principle of presenting separate ideas in separate chunks, rather than nesting new ideas within others. These chunks aren't always sentences, but they do sound distinct enough to help listeners know when Shapiro moves on to a new idea. Even if you write long sentences, fail to finish sentences, or join statements together in unconventional ways, always introduce new ideas one at a time, so listeners aren't burdened with untangling what you're trying to say.

Recapping

Don't expect listeners to remember and refer back to *anything*. Your job as a writer is to hold this information on behalf of the listener. Share it only when required and recap whenever necessary. If you introduce an important component in a story early on, you'll need to return to it regularly to keep it uppermost in listeners' minds. Let's see how this is done in an episode of the *Invisibilia* podcast, a show exploring the invisible forces that shape human behaviour. In this episode, hosts Alix Spiegel and Lulu Miller meet a physicist who researches a phenomenon known as "quantum entanglement".[16]

I'm a physics graduate and I don't know what quantum entanglement means, so it's a safe bet that most listeners won't either. Rather than rushing in with the concept, Spiegel first sets out a visual scene. She explains that she, Miller, and the physicist are standing in front of a huge table covered in lasers and mirrors. Once we know where we are and who we're with (a physicist called David Hucul) Spiegel's then ready to tackle the technicalities:

> And David had brought us to the table because he wanted to use the many lasers and mirrors to try to perform something called quantum entanglement.

Spiegel then explains what quantum entanglement is, in straightforward language that non-physicists can understand:

> He was going to try to take two separate atoms and, using his laser, turn them into the same thing.

We listen as the physicist conducts his experiment and the hosts explain what they see. Once everything's complete, the physicist says:

> So, there's entanglement going on right now between these two chambers.

The other host, Lulu Miller, then steps in and reminds us what entanglement is:

> Those two atoms, East and West, are now one, even though they still sit four feet across from each other on a table.

Later on in the show we realise that quantum entanglement can happen naturally, without the need for lasers. At that point, someone else (journalist Geoff Brumfield) reminds us – again – what entanglement means.

> The idea that two objects that are physically separated, I mean, really physically separated over miles or, you know, eons or whatever – time, space, what have you – are still the same thing is something so foreign …

Though we're repeatedly told what quantum entanglement is, this repetition never feels annoying or unnecessary. The reminders arrive at the precise moments when they're needed, and they're expressed in different ways by different people, so they feel fresh each time.

Visual descriptions

Listeners find it particularly difficult to keep track of multiple pieces of information, so limit the number of names, figures, or technical terms you mention. If you must include numbers, round them up or down, or use analogies to help people visualise what you're talking about. "Simple mindvisible ideas", as playwright Vincent McInerney describes them, help listeners transform what they hear into a memorable, visual scene.[17] For instance, here's Roman Mars, narrator of the *99% Invisible* podcast, sharing an anecdote in an episode about the huge number of birds that die after colliding with buildings.

> The bird collisions that day were especially traumatic for volunteers in downtown Manhattan, particularly those who monitor the new towers at the World Trade Center site. Tower 4 is designed by Japanese architect Fumihiko Maki, and it's known as "Bird Enemy Number One" because of its design. The tower is basically a floor length mirror of a building, and it's in exactly the wrong place.[18]

Mars refers to a site most people will have heard of (the World Trade Center in New York), includes a description that will stick in people's brains (Bird Enemy Number One) and provides a visual reference that's easy to picture (a giant floor-length mirror). It's a quick and effective way to illustrate the impact that buildings make on bird populations, without citing any statistics.

Holding listeners' attention

Some of the best ways to keep listeners engaged are to use simple story structures, offer variety, and create pause and reflect moments.

Simple story structures

The easiest way for listeners to follow a story is if it is set out in a logical, linear form, where the action always moves forward. Never expect the listener to rewind. If listeners need a piece of past information to understand a present action, share it at that moment, rather than trying to incorporate a complex flashback. For instance, the *99% Invisible* story about bird collisions includes a later segment where host Roman Mars talks to a design critic about the bird-friendly design of the Amazon Campus in Virginia. During this discussion, Mars briefly jumps back in time by saying, "Amazon hired a landscape architect named Kate Orff to work on the project, and right away, she noticed the serious problems with the façade." In just one sentence, we get a vital piece of backstory – just when we need it – which helps us to understand why Amazon's building ended up looking as it did.

Variety

If you've ever listened to someone talking to you constantly for 20 minutes or more, you'll know how difficult it can be to stay focused. Successful podcasters make changes within their stories specifically to keep listeners interested. They vary sentence structures, and alter the pace and rhythm of their writing. On a larger scale, they flip to a different perspective, someone else's viewpoint or a physically different location. The key, says *This American Life* host Ira Glass, "is to keep moving between different kinds of moments: funny scenes, emotional scenes, raising questions".[19]

Audio writers can use other tricks too, especially if they incorporate recordings of people and places. Rather than flipping from one person talking in a quiet office to another doing the same, Bill Ash suggests, "let a scene with an indoor acoustic be followed by one out of doors, or a noisy scene at a fairground by a quiet one in somebody's study, or let a scene viewed from inside the mind of one of the characters be followed by a perfectly objective scene from the author's point of view."[20] These changes should, of course, always serve the story. Otherwise, you risk switching things around so much that you lose your listeners.

To spot points where there's a risk of losing your listener, glance through your script. If any parts look like massive, dense blocks of continuous copy, try splitting the narration up or bringing in another perspective.

Pause-and-reflect moments

There will be moments in every story where a listener might naturally need to pause in order to absorb and interpret what they've heard. If you don't pause, too, they'll find it hard to keep up. Build-in opportunities for listeners to stop and reflect via moments of silence or snippets of music. Even a person saying, "Whoa! That's crazy", gives the listener time and a prompt to take stock of the information they just heard.

Sometimes, this pause is made explicit, as in this example from the *Family Secrets* podcast. It comes 17 minutes into a story about Ruthie Lindsay. After Lindsay shares her own description of a complication from spine surgery, narrator Dani Shapiro recaps:

> OK. Let's take a breath or two here. A wire. Had broken. And pierced Ruthie's brainstem.[21]

Shapiro's words are an almost perfect match for Lindsay's. By repeating the words, as if replaying them in slow motion, Shapiro ensures that we pay attention. We recognise the enormity of the situation and reflect on what it means for Lindsay. We may even wonder how she lived to tell the tale.

Signposting

With no headings or paragraph breaks to show when a story pauses or changes direction, audio writers must show listeners what's happening in other ways. Like guiding someone on a walk through an area you know well, audio writers give instructions about which way to go, while highlighting locations of interest. They signal when an important point is made and identify any changes in time or place.

For instance, three-and-a-half minutes into a *This American Life* story about identity theft, journalist Miki Meek says, "This is where Jessamyn's story changes from a garden-variety identity-theft case to something stranger."[22] I won't spoil what comes next, but Meek's interjection suggests that it's not what we expect. Reading a line like this on screen might feel unnecessary. Spoken in a podcast, it tells us that this is a crucial pivot point in the story. It's a signal to pay attention, because everything's about to change.

Writer and graphic artist Jessica Abel says of writing for audio, "sometimes you just really need to state the obvious". If you say, "this is something you really need to know", "that's when things got interesting", or "here's the thing", then listeners know they ought to pay extra attention. This applies equally when changing time or location. For instance, Roman Mars makes a time shift explicit in the *99% Invisible* bird-collision episode by saying, "Kaitlyn Parkins vividly remembers a day last fall that lives in New York birder infamy. October 6th, 2021".

Working with tape

Many of today's story-focused podcasts evolved from stories first told on national public radio stations, like the BBC in the UK and NPR in the US. In NPR podcasts like *This American Life*, stories are built up from narration and "tape".

Tape is another word for an audio recording. In podcast production the term usually applies to recorded interviews that are edited and combined with narration to create the final show. Tape allows listeners to hear from ordinary people involved in the story. People who speak, says Annie Caulfield, "in quirky ways, with passion". Unlike experts trotting out statistics, ordinary people are, says Caulfield, "touching to listen to, unguarded and distinctive".[23]

When you write a story that will be read, you might make use of a limited number of quotes to introduce or back up points that you make, particularly if the quote expresses a thought or idea more effectively than you could. In audio, quotes from other people play a far greater role. Audio stories often have an equal balance between the words the narrator speaks and the words that come from tape.

In many story-based podcasts, tape presents the core of the story. The narrator's role is then to fill in any gaps, provide contextual detail and help listeners transition from one perspective on the story to another. Let's look at how this narration works using an example.

This is an imagined story based on an actual event and the podcast that described it. In this version, the story introduces us to a woman, who we'll call Maria, who witnesses police beating a man on the street and records the event on her cellphone. When Maria calls the police the next day to find out what happened to the man, the police won't share any information.

Narrator: Maria wasn't satisfied with that. She wondered who else she could contact, who else might know what happened.

[This narration gets us thinking about what we might do in a similar situation]

Maria: I talked to my husband, and we thought, why don't we, uh, call the local news – Channel Seven? We used to watch their news every night, at 9 o'clock every night. And we could ask if they knew anything.

Narrator: Channel Seven is ABXY, a major TV station in Seattle.

[This narration gives us contextual detail about Channel Seven and transitions us to the perspective of a broadcast journalist]

Conner: I guess we … we were the top channel then. We prided ourselves on being first to most stories.

Narrator: Jess Conner was the assignment manager at ABXY. If you called the newsroom she usually picked up.

[This narration identifies Conner and her role in the story]

Conner: Maria calls and I answer. She says she has a video of a man being hit by police. So, I said, could you bring it in? And we'll take a look.

Maria: I felt so excited. We were going into the station – Channel Seven. The news department. We hadn't expected that.

Narrator: Jess Conner was one of the first two people at ABXY who watched the video,

[This narration gives us contextual detail, so we understand why Conner's perspective is important. It focuses our attention on what comes next]

Conner: I just couldn't believe it. We always had people sending in video, we'd used some – films that showed people being arrested – but nothing like this. Nothing so awful, so visual ... This was different. We'd never had anything like it before.

Narrator: The ABXY news team immediately got to work. Conner brought in the station's star reporter, Fred Hampton.

[This narration again provides contextual detail, which helps us understand the enormity of the story]

Maria: Fred was the reporter we liked best, so we were, like, a bit starstruck, really.

Narrator: Within the hour, Hampton and a cameraman were at Maria's apartment. The interview took under ten minutes.

[This narration bridges a brief gap in the events of the story]

Maria: We couldn't wait to tell everyone we were going to be on the news. We called our friends and, yeah, told them all to watch.

Narrator: Maria didn't think about the consequences of broadcasting her video on a major news channel. She was just excited to be on TV. ABXY's senior news editors did think about it though. They had something powerful and they knew it. Here's ABXY News director Brad Chesney.

[This narration helps us transition from the facts of the story to the issues behind it. We start thinking about the possible consequences of broadcasting the video recording and are introduced to an important decision maker in the story]

Chesney: Well, we needed to be very careful. We just, you know, didn't want to fire things up. It's a minefield ... Sure as hell there's no guidebook for handling this sort of thing.

Narrator: On Tuesday, March 25th, 1993, Maria's film was broadcast for the first time on ABXY's 9 o'clock news.[24]

[This narration acts like a cliffhanger chapter ending. We're primed for what comes next]

Like a close-up in a movie, tape zooms into the midst of the action, helping us appreciate what happened from the perspective of someone who was there – or, at least, someone who has a more insightful view of events than the narrator. In podcasts that incorporate a lot of tape, your role as a writer is to select appropriate extracts, patch them together to tell the story, and insert narration only where needed. While you could do this simply by looking at transcripts of the tape, listening to it allows you to spot anything that might sound weird to a listener, or anything that breaks up the rhythm of the piece.

Presenting your audio script

When you finish drafting, revising, and editing a text-based story, it doesn't usually change. Once it's published, readers see the words you placed in the story, arranged and presented as you (and your editor) decided. When you write an audio story, the end-point isn't the finished story, but a script.

When the host or narrator reads the script during recording, they may make small adjustments, pause in places you hadn't considered, or emphasise unexpected phrases. This can happen even if you record your own words.

While changes made at the recording stage should enhance the finished product, you may want to guide the narrator to read the story in the way you intended. For instance, you might include in your script:

- Instructions about how you want it to be read. You could be explicit about when you expect a pause or underline words you want emphasised.
- Phonetic spellings for unusual words so they are pronounced as you intend. Most dictionaries provide phonetic spellings if you need them. Be sure to check that the phonetic spelling refers to the version of English used in your country.

It's also worth thinking about how a script is physically used during a recording. You don't want the speaker to lose momentum because of a page turn, or lose their place if individual pages are placed out of order. That's why I always format scripts by:

- Including page numbers in a consistent position on the page, printed in a large font – so they're easy to see.
- Making sure that page breaks don't split a piece of running text onto separate pages. I place the page break at a moment when there is a natural pause, so it doesn't interrupt the speaker. This also makes it easy to remove any distracting page-turn sounds during the audio edit, since they'll be separate from any narration.

Once you've drafted your script, you're ready for the final part of any writing process: revision and editing, which we'll cover in the next chapter.

Summary

- Listeners expect to feel a connection with the narrator or host of a podcast.
- Audio stories lack the visual cues that readers rely on to help them understand where they are in a story and when the story flips to a new time or location.

- Listeners must absorb, understand, and reflect on a story at a pace dictated by the narrator.
- It can be particularly difficult for listeners to keep track of multiple pieces of information, like names, numbers, and technical terms.
- Common ways of opening a podcast include posing a question, introducing a mystery, outlining a big idea, describing a physical location, bringing a key moment to life, or meeting the host.
- In some nonfiction storytelling podcasts, recorded interviews (known as tape) tell the bulk of the story.
- An audio script is not the finished story product. It will be adapted and performed when it is recorded.

Practical lessons for audio writers

- **Write as you would speak.** Use simple words and short, active sentences. Write in fragmented sentences if that makes sense, but present separate ideas in distinct phrases, so everything's easy to follow.
- **Be yourself.** Use language you would say in everyday conversation and make a conscious effort to reveal your personality.
- **Use a simple, linear structure.** Never expect the listener to rewind. Keep the action moving forward in a logical order. Avoid flashbacks if you can.
- **Focus on holding your listener's interest.** Don't overload listeners with information. Share only what they need to know when they need it. Recap key points throughout the story if necessary.
- **Take extra care to help readers understand where they are in a story.** Be explicit about transitions between times, places, or perspectives.
- **Emphasise vital plot points.** If there's a crucial moment, which everything else relies on, tell readers that this is where everything changes.
- **Provide opportunities for processing and reflection.** Build in moments where listeners can take stock of what they've heard. You might include blocks of silence, snippets of music, or comments from the narrator.
- **Guide listeners through the tape.** If you're building a story from tape, use narration to fill in any gaps, provide contextual detail, and help listeners transition from one moment or viewpoint to another.
- **Annotate your script.** Indicate where the narrator should pause or give emphasis, and how unfamiliar terms should be pronounced.

Recommended reading

Jessica Abel, *Out On the Wire: The Storytelling Secrets of the New Masters of Radio* (New York: Crown Publishing Group, 2015) – detailed exploration of how shows like *This American Life* source, script, and produce podcast stories, beautifully depicted in the form of a graphic novel.

Jules Horne, *Writing for Audiobooks: Audio-first for Flow and Impact: Author Advice from Radio Writing* (Kelso: Method Writing, 2020) – practical advice for writing and recording an audiobook.

Notes and references

1　Jules Horne, *Writing for Audiobooks: Audio-first for Flow and Impact: Author Advice from Radio Writing* (Kelso: Method Writing, 2020)

2　Kevin Anderson, and Colin Gray, *Engaging Episodes: Creating Powerful Podcast Content: Creating Audio Programmes that Inspire Fanatical Fans* (Wild Trails Media: 2016)

3　David Greene, "How NPR's David Greene Learned a New 'Art Form' in Radio", NPR, 6 December 2017 <https://training.npr.org/2017/12/06/how-nprs-david-greene-learned-a-new-art-form-in-radio/> (accessed 10 February 2023)

4　Kevin Anderson, and Colin Gray, *Engaging Episodes*

5　Alison MacAdam, "How Audio Stories Begin", NPR Training, 26 July 2016 <https://training.npr.org/2016/07/26/how-audio-stories-begin/> (accessed 9 March 2023)

6　Mukti Jain Campion, "Maidens' Voyage", *Departures*, podcast, 2021, a Culture Wise production for the Migration Museum <https://www.migrationmuseum.org/output/audio/departures-podcast-episode-2-maidens-voyage/> (accessed 27 April 2023)

7　Anna Faherty and Judith Watts, "The Sign of the Penguins", *Bookshapers*, podcast, 20 May 2022 <https://bookshapers.co.uk/podcast/the-sign-of-the-penguins/> (accessed 11 March 2023)

8　Allison Behringer + KCRW, "Refusing to Feed", *Bodies*, podcast, 3 October 2018 <https://www.bodiespodcast.com/resource-pages/2018/8/28/episode-3-anxious-mess-mxm4r-sb32f> (accessed 8 June 2023)

9　Wondery, "Trick or Treat", *Stolen Hearts*, podcast, 6 February 2023 <https://wondery.com/shows/stolen-hearts/episode/12149-trick-or-treat/> (accessed 8 June 2023)

10　Emily Silverman, "On Trial", *Shame in Medicine: The Lost Forest*, podcast, 25 October 2022 <https://www.thenocturnists-shame.org/episodes/7-on-trial> (accessed 8 June 2023)

11　William Ash, *The Way to Write Radio Drama* (London: Elm Tree Books, 1985)

12　Annie Caulfield, *Writing for Radio: A Practical Guide* (Marlborough, Wilts: The Crowood Press, 2009)

13　Meta, "Marc Fennell on Stuff the British Stole", Meta, 2 December 2020 <https://play.acast.com/s/meta/marcfennellons0074uffthebritishstole> (accessed 10 January 2023)

14　Alison MacAdam, "The Journey from Print to Radio Storytelling: A Guide for Navigating a New Landscape", *NPR*, 6 December 2017 <https://training.npr.org/2017/12/06/the-journey-from-print-to-radio-storytelling-a-guide-for-navigating-a-new-landscape/> (accessed 9 February 2023)

15　Dani Shapiro, "Open Secrets", *Family Secrets*, podcast, February 2019

16 NPR, "Mirror Touch", *Invisibilia*, podcast, 30 January 2015 <https://www.npr.org/2015/01/30/382453493/mirror-touch NPR> (accessed 8 June 2023)

17 Vincent McInerney, *Writing for Radio* (Manchester: Manchester University Press, 2001)

18 Roman Mars, "Murder Most Fowl", *99% Invisible*, podcast, 4 May 2022 <https://99percentinvisible.org/episode/murder-most-fowl/transcript> (accessed 8 March 2023), produced by Chris Berube and Alexandra Lange

19 Jessica Abel, *Out On the Wire: The Storytelling Secrets of the New Masters of Radio* (New York: Crown Publishing Group, 2015)

20 William Ash, *The Way to Write Radio Drama*

21 Dani Shapiro, "The Wire", *Family Secrets*, podcast, October 2020

22 Miki Meek, "The Haunted Becomes the Haunter" story in the episode "Same Bed, Different Dreams", *This American Life*, podcast, 25 September 2020 <https://www.thisamericanlife.org/556/same-bed-different-dreams/act-three-10> (accessed 6 March 2023)

23 Annie Caulfield, *Writing for Radio*

24 This ficticious example is inspired by Joel Anderson's script about George Holliday's videotape of the beating of Rodney King in LA in 1991, as heard in "The Tape", *Slow Burn: The LA Riots*, podcast, 3 November 2021 <https://slate.com/podcasts/slow-burn/s6/the-la-riots/e1/george-hollidays-video-of-the-rodney-king-beating-changed-everything> (accessed 8 March 2023)

8 Reviewing, editing, and publishing your story

This chapter focuses on reviewing your draft and preparing your story for publication. Full of valuable checklists, it's designed to help you improve your writing, while producing a consistent, accurate, and engaging story. The chapter covers:

- How to read and revise your first draft
- Fact checking
- Obtaining permission to reproduce other people's content
- Taking care of yourself and your sources
- Final pre-publication checks

Whenever I teach writing, there's one part of the process that flummoxes students more than any other: the need to review and revise their work. It's no surprise that many students overlook this. After all, when we speak, we simply say what's on our mind. When we send an SMS or IM, we ping our words out the second they come into our heads.

There's much to be said for getting your writing out there with similar haste. Your unfiltered words will sound immediate and authentic, and you won't waste hours second-guessing yourself. However, the form in which your writing ideas first come to you is rarely the form that makes most sense to a reader or listener. If you want your words to have impact, to be received as you intended, and to drive the action you seek, revision is key. Going, "the extra mile and then a few more" is, say journalist Mark Kramer and writer Wendy Call, what transforms a "plain ol' writer" into a good one.[1]

As cognitive psychologist Steven Pinker writes in his book *The Sense of Style*, "too many things have to go right in a passage of writing for most mortals to get them all the first time".[2] According to Pinker, our brains lack capacity to complete every part of the writing process in one go. So, we need to work in phases. Phase 1 involves thinking about why you're writing and what you want to say. Phase 2 is when you wrangle words onto the page. Only then can you free up

DOI: 10.4324/9781003363347-10

fresh brain space for phase 3: transforming your draft into a clear, elegant, engaging story. Giving yourself time to pause, revisit, and check your work also reduces the risk of publishing something inflammatory, inaccurate, or ill-advised.

This final chapter begins with step-by-step guidelines for reading and revising your draft story. It then outlines the most vital pre-publication tasks, including fact checking, clearing copyright, and the final read-through. By the time you reach the end of the chapter, you should be ready to launch a well-crafted story into the world, safe in the knowledge that you've done everything you could to refine and polish it.

Gaining fresh perspectives

If you're writing for a publication or organisation that will edit your submission, the reviewing stage prepares your story for your editor's wise interventions. If you're publishing a story yourself, the responsibility for getting everything publication-ready rests solely with you. This is far from ideal. Writers are generally so deeply entwined with their work that they find it difficult to edit from a fresh – objective – perspective. If you usually work alone, try one or more of these tactics to open up a new perspective.

- Create distance from your writing by leaving it untouched for as long as possible. When you revisit your draft, print it out. This forces you to look anew at what you've dealt with on screen.
- Pair up with a writing buddy – someone who may read and feedback on your drafts in return for you reading theirs.
- Gather together a group of people interested in or knowledgeable about the subject of your story and ask them to become beta readers. Like beta testers for software, they'll road test your early drafts.

When you receive comments from readers, editors, or technical experts, be prepared for criticism. This isn't, says *Washington Post* reporter Anne Hull, "a time to protect your ego".[3] It's a time to listen. Heed what people tell you, even if you choose not to act on every piece of advice they share. Don't take things personally. Read your story as if it were written by a stranger, and advocate for your readers and listeners. Delete words or sections that mean something to you, but serve little purpose for them. Challenge anything that confuses, obstructs, or offends.

Reading and revising your draft

Revising your story involves five key activities, best completed in this order.

1 Reading and revising **for story.** Checking that your story has all the required ingredients and all the information your audience needs. This process is sometimes described as a structural edit.

2 Reading and revising **for inclusion.** Checking that nothing might exclude or offend any audiences. This is sometimes described as a sensitivity read.
3 Reading and revising **for accuracy.** Checking facts and verifying evidence.
4 Reading and revising **for clarity.** Checking that everything makes sense for your reader or listener. This and reading for style are sometimes described as line editing, copy-editing, or subediting.
5 Reading and revising **for style.** Checking that your writing delivers a smooth and engaging read or listen, by redrafting clunky sentences, removing unnecessary words, and standardising tone. This also involves checking spelling and punctuation.

Each of these strategies is summarised in one of the sections below, where you'll also find handy checklists. If you're tempted to combine everything into one task, think about creating a combined revision checklist, so you don't miss anything. Always prioritise the first task (looking at your story from a structural perspective) before making any edits to individual words and sentences.

Reading for story

The first stage of reviewing and revising any draft is to focus on story structure. There's little point finessing individual words before the structure is sound. Start by reviewing the overall story and the order in which you introduce information. Read your draft in full and ask yourself the following questions. Even better, ask someone else to review your story with these questions in mind.

1 Does it make you *feel* anything?
2 Have you included all the story ingredients? Is there a relatable person, a challenge, a specific setting, visual and contextual detail, a sequence of events, and a resolution?
3 Does the resolution resolve the challenge?
4 Does the sequence of events lead directly from the challenge to the resolution?
5 Are you answering your reader's or listener's questions? Do you reveal who the story is about, where and when it takes place, what happens, and why?
6 Does every section move the storyline on?

If you answered no to any of these questions, make changes to improve the focus and structure. This may highlight unnecessary passages that you feel very attached to; be firm with yourself and cut them if they play no role in advancing the story.

Consider, also, whether the story works for your ideal reader or listener, and whether it supports your story purpose. Revisit the work you completed in Chapters 1 and 4 to evaluate these aspects.

If you struggle to make the structure work, reuse the tools introduced in Chapter 5. Try listing out all the story events – in words or on Post-Its – to spot whether anything's missing or extraneous. Think about how the story might be improved if it started or ended elsewhere. Only when you're confident in your structure should you move on.

Reading for inclusion

In this stage of the reading and revision process, you'll need to:

• Recognise and acknowledge your own unconscious bias.
• Portray people, events, settings, and beliefs in a sensitive, culturally appropriate way.
• Identify and remove language that offends.
• Identify and remove language that reinforces damaging societal structures.

As discussed in Chapter 6, if you're writing about a group of people to which you don't belong, you won't have the best grasp on cultural sensitivities and appropriate language. This is why book publishers often employ sensitivity or authenticity readers. If you're recruiting a group of beta readers yourself, be sure to include stakeholders from any communities you're writing about.

Unconscious bias

While we all like to think we're moral people who write stories based on objective research, each of us is prone to an intrinsic bias that causes us to rate people similar to us more highly than someone who is, in some way, different. This *unconscious bias* arises when your brain makes automatic associations between specific groups of people and certain characteristics – stereotypes that aren't usually true.[4] We don't spot these biases because they're a product of invisible systems that, as Rebecca Solnit writes, were, "constructed by people who analysed and argued and shifted our assumptions".[5]

Because you're unaware of it, unconscious bias can pervade your writing without you realising. Here are some symptoms to diagnose your own bias.

1 **Language that labels.** For instance, why tell us one person in your story is Black or transgender if you don't point out that another is white or cisgender? This doesn't mean you shouldn't mention someone's race, religion, gender, or sexuality if it's relevant, simply that you shouldn't label them in this way if the information plays no role in the story.
2 **Language that reinforces stereotypes.** For instance, using terms stereotypically associated with specific genders, like "emotional" (for a woman) and "driven" (for a man). If you're not sure whether you do this, ask yourself whether you would use the same word to describe the same action taken by someone of a different gender, race, religion, or sexuality.

3 **Language that judges.** For example, writing that someone "lost their battle with cancer". This might suggest that you consider the person to have failed in some way – because they didn't "win" the fight.
4 **Language that excludes.** For example, jargon or acronyms that aren't recognised outside a specific field or group. Phrases like "there's no need to spell it out" may also exclude people who lack the requisite knowledge to understand what you're talking about.

Authenticity, sensitivity, and inclusion

Here are some of the most effective ways to ensure that you tell an authentic, culturally sensitive, and inclusive story.

1 Ask someone from the community that you're writing about to read and feed back on your story. Even better, work with them while you research and develop it.
2 Respect the language people use to describe themselves.
3 Follow reporting guidelines and codes of conduct published by organisations like the National Union of Journalists (in the UK), the Media, Entertainment & Arts Alliance (in Australia), and the American Society of Journalists and Authors.
4 Be open to challenge, ready to learn about others' experiences, and willing to reflect on your own biases.

Reading for accuracy

While nonfiction writers ought to be researching, checking, and verifying facts as they develop their story, the review stage is the last chance to double-check everything. From spotting inadvertent typing errors to verifying potentially inaccurate sources, this process can take up a huge amount of time. At a basic level, reviewing for accuracy involves checking aspects like:

1 **Names, titles, place names.** Are they spelled correctly? Are you using the currently accepted names of historical people and locations?
2 **Times, distances, dates, locations, historical facts.** Are they accurate?
3 **Statistics.** Are they accurate and relevant?
4 **Facts hidden within descriptions.** For instance, if you say "she had six symptoms", which you then go on to list in full, check that there are, indeed, six. If you write, "she travelled east towards Baghdad", double-check that east is an accurate description, based on the starting point. If you tell us something happened on Sunday 22 May 1975, check that May 22 in that year fell on a Sunday.
5 **Superlatives.** Do you have evidence to support statements like "the first", "the only", or "the most"?

The need for scepticism

While checks like those listed above ensure that your writing reflects what you've researched, they may fail to pick up every inaccuracy. Even when you've spoken to a person or checked a document, your sources may not reflect what actually happened. Reasons for this include:

- **Urban myths.** Some entirely fictional stories or anecdotes are so convincing that people believe them to be true. When they reinforce our world view, we circulate them widely and they become accepted as common knowledge.
- **Faulty memories.** We've all been tricked by our memory at some point, thinking we saw, said, or heard something that didn't happen, at least not in the same way we remember it.
- **Contested histories.** Even when someone feels certain about what they saw or experienced, others may view what happened through a different lens. The "truth" depends on who you are and how you interpret a situation.
- **Lost context.** When you focus in on a specific moment in a story, you lose the context around it. For instance, if I tell you I saw a young, shaven-headed man running up to an older man in a suit and grabbing hold of him, you may well conclude that the older man was being mugged. If I tell you that I also saw a pile of bricks about to fall on the older man, and that the young man pulled him out of their path, you'll realise this was a rescue. Without that additional context, your interpretation of events is inaccurate.[6]
- **Overlooked context.** Sometimes the context is available, but we miss it. For instance, if you find a historical photograph of a person or location, but fail to spot its age, you might inadvertently present it as a current image.
- **Manipulation.** We all make selections about what we include or exclude when we tell stories. However, sometimes people select and edit information or media with the deliberate aim of misrepresenting the truth.
- **Staging.** Some content may be planned or staged. Think of the silly videos you see online – of people who appear to accidentally trip over an item in their house in spectacular fashion. How many do you think are true accidents?
- **Artificially generated content.** Artificial intelligence may be used to generate words or media that sound or look real. Deepfake content recreates the face, voice, and movements of a real person, giving the impression that a computer-generated video or audio piece is an authentic recording.

All this highlights the importance of working through a structured fact-checking process.

Fact checking

Full Fact, a team of independent fact checkers and campaigners, describes the process of fact checking like this: "take claims, trace them, and weigh the evidence available".[7] Like researching evidence when writing an academic essay, fact checking requires critical thinking. You need to find the original source of a claim, corroborate whether it's accurate, and consider why it was made or shared. Sifting the most relevant and important evidence from a mass of information also plays a role.

This seven-point checklist provides a useful starting point for responsible fact checking.

1 **Be sceptical.** Assume everything could be false until you find corroborating evidence to suggest otherwise.
2 **Keep an open mind.** Be humble and modest about what you know, or what you assume to be true.
3 **Check everything.** As the American Press Institute says, when journalists get their facts wrong it's usually because they failed to check information sourced from someone else.[8] Apply the same standard to every claim and keep asking yourself "How do I know that?"
4 **Use your common sense.** Reflect on whether you'd expect to see or hear this information elsewhere. For instance, if it really were true, wouldn't there be a news report, or other traceable consequences?
5 **Use the best available primary sources.** Find the first instance of publication or, if people have shared information with you, ask them "How do you know that?"
6 **Search for corroborating evidence.** Seek out other witnesses to the same event and check whether their descriptions match. Look for relevant documentary evidence or video or audio footage.
7 **Consider motivations.** Identify the source of the information and consider what that person or organisation might have to gain by sharing it.

When you list out all the different aspects involved in fact checking it can feel overwhelming. The best way to manage this is to do what journalists do and make fact checking a habit. Journalists pose questions as they research their story, documenting every item of evidence they gather. If they lack evidence, or are uncertain about some aspects of their story, they're transparent about it.

Communicating uncertainty

Though it's good practice to be explicit about uncertainty, this transparency has an unfortunate side-effect. Humans have a natural aversion to ambiguity, which makes us trust data that feels definite and unwavering over anything that feels less certain. Talking about uncertainty has much in common with tiptoeing along a tightrope – put one foot wrong and all is lost.

One simple tactic for reducing the mistrust associated with ambiguity is to specify where uncertainty lies and why. Explain the reasons for any evidence gaps in your story, identify your sources (if you're able to) and flag their likely biases. If citing estimated numbers, give the range the estimate falls within, like this: "The estimated cost is around $10.4m (between $10m and $10.8m)". If you're confident sharing your own research process – and links to sources – do so. This can help readers or listeners appreciate why some aspects of your story remain ambiguous.[9] Some storytellers make a virtue of this, as Sarah Koenig did during the *Serial* podcast (which we met in Chapter 3). Koenig continually shared what she knew, what she couldn't deduce, and what she wasn't sure of, 'facts' which often changed between episodes.

Reading for clarity

With a sound structure and your facts in order you can focus on reading each scene for clarity. Look for moments where your reader or listener could become confused – by individual words and phrases, ambiguous information, or omission. Because you know the story and the topic, it's all too easy to leave something out even if it's vital for readers and listeners. A reader who doesn't know the story can really help here. They'll tell you where they felt lost or where they needed to revisit sections to grasp your meaning.

When reading for clarity, ask yourself questions like:

1   Does the reader or listener have all the information they need to follow my train of thought?
2   Is every section and sentence clear?
3   Is every word or phrase unambiguous?
4   Have I defined any jargon, acronyms, or abbreviations?
5   Do I understand the meaning of every word I've used?

If you answered no to any of these questions, make changes to improve clarity. This may involve inserting additional information or removing confused phrases. If you realise you need a modifier (like an adjective or adverb) to alter the meaning of a word, chances are, you don't have the right word. Relinquish the modifier and swap the original for a precise alternative instead.

If you have a call to action, check this for clarity too. If readers or listeners don't understand what you want them to do, your ultimate goal may never be achieved.

Dealing with data

If your story includes numerical data, think about whether this serves the purpose you intend. Many readers or listeners find numbers difficult to grasp, particularly if you're talking about massive quantities like billions. Numerical evidence you value may therefore fail to make an impression, so consider expressing this information in words instead.

Reading for style

When you have a clear, well-structured story, you can read and revise for style. This is the most mentally demanding part of the editing process. Paying attention as you "inch your way through every sentence, word for word" requires serious concentration.[10] Start by checking your spelling and grammar. Look for lines that sound clunky and paragraphs that outstay their welcome. Search for "-ly" words and "was" as signals of unnecessary modifiers or a passive tone. If you're aware of your own bad writing habits, look for these too. Build on this by asking yourself:

1 Are there any long-winded phrases or sentences, which will be difficult to read or hear?
2 Are there any redundant words or phrases?
3 Are too many of my sentences the same length?
4 Do I (unintentionally) repeat the same word several times in a single sentence or paragraph?
5 Have I used clichés?
6 Are there places where showing would be more impactful than telling?
7 Are there places where telling would work more effectively than showing?
8 Does my mix of events and detail feel out of balance?
9 Could I add in any sensory detail?
10 Could I vary the pace?
11 Could my phrasing be more active and direct?
12 Could I use quotes or media to augment my words?

If you answered yes to any of these questions, make changes to improve your style. This may involve introducing variety – in terms of word choice, sentence length, and pace – while ensuring consistency.

Listening

At this stage, it's worth focusing on how your writing *sounds*. Whether your audience will be listening or reading, the sound of your words impacts their experience. Read your story out loud – and I mean out loud; don't just mouth the words in silence. Listen to what you hear. Is the tone appropriate? Are there moments when tone or pace shift unintentionally? Do you, as author Rebecca McClanahan asks "use soft, soothing consonants in one description and harsh, cacophonous consonants in another?"[11] Do the pace and tone match the actions that they're describing? Could you use devices like alliteration (where consecutive words start with the same sound) or onomatopoeia (where the sound of a word reflects its meaning) to enhance the sound of your story? If so, do this sparingly – these approaches become distracting if overused.

Overall, your story should sound "on brand". If it doesn't sound like you (or the slice of you you're sharing with readers and listeners), make changes.

Cutting

If you find yourself really stuck with a word, a sentence, or even an entire section, reflect on whether you could cut it. Often the solution to an editing problem isn't to rewrite but to remove what wasn't working.

Cutting is a painful process yet, as William Zinsser says, "most first drafts can be cut by 50 per cent without losing any information or losing the author's voice". When I work as an editor, writer's drafts that fit the word count often end up way under length because I cut so much. Worse, because the writer was so focused on not running over, they omitted useful information and colourful detail. At first-draft stage, rich, overlong copy is far preferable than wishy-washy text that shrinks uncomfortably during the edit. The corollary of this is, of course, that you as a writer must be prepared to make substantial cuts to your own work. As a starting point, follow Joseph M Williams's list of actions designed to deliver writing with "grace":

1 Delete words that add nothing to the meaning, like cutting "certain"'from the phrase "certain factors influence".
2 Delete words that mean the same as another word, like cutting "full" from the phrase "a full and complete edit".
3 Delete words that say what readers can infer, like cutting "true" from the phrase "she outlined the true facts".
4 Replace a phrase with a word if you can, like using "because" instead of "due to the fact that".
5 Change negatives to affirmatives, like using "rarely" instead of "not often".[12]

If you make any cuts, be sure to set your story aside and read it one more time before moving on. On this reading you may realise you've been over-zealous. If you spot a cut that causes confusion, sacrifices meaning, or interrupts the flow, reinstate what you removed. This cutting, checking, reinstating process can feel like a tug of war between your draft and the final story. Alternatively, King Kurus of the *Black History Buff* podcast likens working with phrases that drift in and out of a story to "sculpting with clouds".[13]

Consistency

Varied word choices and changes in pace will improve your writing. However, consistency also has value. It helps keep your reader or listener with you by removing distractions. For instance, if you spell filmmaker without a hyphen at the start of your story, drop the hyphen in all other mentions. If you tell us the time is 10pm, don't say an hour later that it's 23:00. If you italicise a book title on first mention, italicise it every time the title appears.

When making decisions about how to spell or present a word, you'll often find two or more perfectly acceptable options. That's when style guides can be useful.

Style reference sources

If you're not careful, you can spend an inordinate amount of time pondering questions around grammar, spelling, and the appropriate use of everything from abbreviations to hyphenation and italics. Authoritative reference sources, like those shown in Table 8.1, can therefore save you precious editing time.

One of my favourite writing buddies is a strange beast: a dictionary that omits every definition. Not sure whether it's browseable or browsable? Whether hyperventilate should be hyper-ventilate? Whether the plural of thesaurus is thesauri or thesauruses? My spelling dictionary gives me recommendations in a second (in these cases: browsable, hyperventilate, and either). While programs

Table 8.1 Style reference sources for writers and editors

To ...	Use a ...
check spelling	**spelling dictionary** For British English I use the printed *New Oxford Spelling Dictionary*, an alphabetised list of words without definitions.
check meaning	**dictionary** There are plenty of printed and online options. Oxford (for British English) and Merriam-Webster (for American English) are two of the most respected brands. Each offers a range of formats and subject coverage, including multivolume editions.
find alternative words	**thesaurus** I use thesaurus.com, but there are plenty of printed and online options, including one offered by Merriam-Webster.
understand grammar and punctuation, how to present numbers, when to italicise and more	**writing and editing handbooks** The pocket-sized *New Hart's Rules* (for British English) is one of the most used. For more comprehensive coverage, Judith Butcher's *Copy-editing* (for British English) and *The Chicago Manual of Style* (for American English) are indispensable. Both are substantial enough to double as doorstops.
check abbreviations, symbols, capitalisation and more	**style guides** Many publications and organisations develop their own style guides. If you're working with a client, ask for a copy of theirs. Alternatively, consult one freely available online, like those produced by the BBC and the US Government Publishing Office.[14] You might even develop a bespoke style guide as a record of your personal writing decisions.

like MS Word provide suggestions on these issues too, a printed source serves as an unchanging reference source, which I can return to if I ever need to check (or back up) my editorial decisions.

Whether you consult a reference source or not, you'll end up making style decisions as you write. If you note them down, you'll build a bespoke style guide for you or your client. As an example, here are some of the style decisions I noted down while writing this book:

- *Spelling:* British English, -ise (not -ize).
- *Quotes:* Double quotes for quotations: "quote here", single quotes for quotes within quotes: "she said it was 'a quote' though I didn't believe her".
- *Numbers:* one to ten spelled out; 11 and up in numerals.
- *Dates:* 15 May 1930.
- *Bullets:* capitalise each first word, full stop at end of each bullet.
- *Book and podcast titles:* italicised.
- *Spellings:* Black (capital B)/copy-editing (hyphen)/MS Word (not Microsoft Word)/nonfiction (no hyphen)/short form (no hyphen, unless used as an adjective).

Handling copyright

Copyright is a legal right that protects content creators like writers and artists. It gives you (the writer) the exclusive right to reproduce, distribute, adapt, or sell your own writing. If other people reproduce your words without obtaining permission from you, they infringe your copyright.

As soon as a piece of content has been recorded in some way, copyright arises automatically. If you have an idea in your head, it won't be subject to copyright. If you write your idea down, or record yourself saying it, you've captured the idea in a tangible form and copyright applies. Though copyright exists without you doing anything else, in some countries you may only be able to defend your rights in court if you formally register your content.[15]

The initial copyright owner is usually you – the content creator – but if you produced material while employed by an organisation, or when working for a client, they may own the copyright instead. You can check this by consulting the wording in your contract; look out for clauses titled "copyright", "intellectual property (IP)", or "rights".

Identifying copyright material

If you want to include extracts of other people's writing in your own work, or images or other media from third-party sources, you may need to gain permission to use this content. To gauge whether permission is needed:

1 **Identify material that may be subject to copyright.** Note any content (words, images, or other media) within your story that you didn't create yourself.

2 **Find the original sources of this content.** Identify the author or creator, the original publisher, and the first date of publication.
3 **Check whether the content is protected by copyright.** Consult authoritative sources in your own country to find out which copyright rules apply. For instance, in the UK and US, the gov.uk and copyright.gov websites state that most written works are protected during the lifetime of the author and for 70 years after their death (though there are exceptions).[16]

If you realise that the material you want to use is subject to copyright, ask yourself whether you really need it. Perhaps you could rephrase the information in your own words? Or, if your end-product includes hyperlinks, simply link to this information rather than reproducing it *within* the story.

If this material feels essential, you'll need to request permission to use it. Don't be fooled into thinking that because you're publishing online, or because you've seen other people use the same material, then copyright doesn't apply. Though copyright can be a legal grey area, each of the uses below is likely to infringe copyright unless you have received permission from the copyright holder.

- **Embedding images and videos.** Though you're not uploading the image to your site, you are *reproducing* it within your story.
- **Reading someone's written words aloud.** Copyright prevents you reproducing someone else's content in any media, even if that's different to the format in which it was originally published.
- **Changing one or two words in a quote or making small edits to an image.** This doesn't mask the fact that you're using someone else's content.
- **Only including a few of someone else's words.** This is particularly true if you want to use song lyrics or a memorable line of poetry or prose. These are notoriously difficult (and expensive) to license.
- **Including content you have seen on other websites.** Even if someone else has infringed copyright, the copyright still exists.
- **Including images classified as "public domain" in other territories.** Copyright laws across the world work on different principles. Always check the rules in your own location.

In most countries there are some legal exceptions to copyright. These allow people to reuse copyright material without permission in a few, specific circumstances. Details vary, so it's always worth consulting the website of the copyright office in your country to find out more.

Clearing permissions

If in doubt, it's best to ask for permission. Contact the copyright owner and make a formal request for permission to reproduce their content in your story.

In some cases you may need to do substantial investigative work to unearth who owns or manages the copyright. The copyright holder might be the original author or artist, a publisher or gallery, their agent, or – in the case of someone who has died – whoever manages their estate. For audio recordings it may be the person speaking or the person who made the recording.

Once you've tracked down the owner, your permissions request ought to include:

- **Details of the content you want to reproduce** and where it was first published (e.g. "I would like to reproduce 254 words from the article 'XYZ', published by ABC.com on 24 March 2025"). Aim to include the title, author, publisher, date of publication, and – if published online – a weblink.
- **A copy of the content you want to reproduce**, for example, the full extract you want to use or a copy of the image or audio file.
- **Information about where and how you will reproduce the content** (e.g. "in a 1,200-word Substack newsletter article about X, entitled CDF"). Contextual information that shows how you will introduce or comment on the content – or any edits or amendments you intend to make – helps the copyright owner to gauge whether they're comfortable with your plans. This includes informing the copyright holder if you intend to translate their words or crop or recolour an image.
- **Information about how you will distribute the content** (e.g. "This will be made available online on xyz.com, for free, from April 2026"). Give information about the publishing location, the date and price (if there is one), and the number of people you expect to access your story.
- **The rights you require** (e.g. "commercial, non-exclusive, worldwide English language rights in all forms and media, including in print and online"). Think about all the circumstances in which your story will be shared and ensure you have covered all eventualities.
- **Your contact details.**

Unless you know a copyright holder personally, clearing permissions can be a laborious process. Pre-emptive copyright licences can streamline this process for both copyright holders and the people who want to use their content.

Pre-emptive licences

Pre-emptive copyright licences are free, easy-to-use agreements that grant permission for anyone to use a work protected by copyright. They are useful tools for sharing your own writing or when reproducing content from other sources.

If you apply a pre-emptive licence to your own writing, you automatically give people permission to use it. This saves the end-user time, because they don't need to request permission. It saves you time too, since you won't need to respond to permissions requests.

Creative Commons (CC) have developed a set of pre-emptive licences that include standardised descriptions to indicate the specific terms of use. For instance, you might choose to release your content under a CC licence that requires you to be identified as the creator of the work, or a licence that says your work may not be adapted.

The online writer's duty of care

Once your story is out in the world, it will impact your readers or listeners, the people you have written about and you. As a writer, you have a duty of care to each of these groups. While there are legal aspects for nonfiction writers to consider, such as copyright, libel, and defamation, you'll encounter ethical questions about how to present and share other people's stories too.

To gauge what's appropriate, you may find it useful to consult and follow professional codes of conduct, like those developed by national journalist associations. I have drawn on these codes in the suggested lists of ethical practice below. If you're ever unsure about whether your actions are ethical, consult the code of your local association and/or discuss your decisions with a trusted colleague.

Readers and listeners

Readers and listeners deserve accuracy and responsible reporting. They should feel included and protected from the moment they spot your content (e.g. your title, first line, and any imagery) in their social media feed. Your duty of care therefore extends to potential readers and listeners too.

This checklist sets out seven key principles of ethical writing for online readers and listeners.

1 Do strive to disclose and interpret information in an honest, accurate, fair, and transparent manner.
2 Do distinguish between fact and opinion.
3 Do provide a balanced view, identify your biases and acknowledge alternative perspectives on an issue.
4 Do provide contextual detail so readers and listeners have the full picture and may draw their own conclusions about disputed events.
5 Don't promote or glamorise potentially dangerous behaviour.
6 Don't share content that could lead to discrimination or hatred, e.g. on the grounds of someone's age, gender, race, colour, religion, disability, marital status, or sexual orientation.
7 Be aware that some language or content may cause distress to readers or listeners who have experienced traumatic events in the past. Consider using content or trigger warnings.

Sources and subjects

The people you're writing about deserve to be treated with respect. While representing them fairly and honestly, think, also, about the impact that your story might have on them. Follow these principles if you can.

1 Ask for permission to tell someone else's story. Make them aware of the potential consequences, so they can take an informed decision. Be aware that power differentials and privilege may play a role here. For instance, if a doctor asks a patient for permission to tell their story, the patient may feel unable to say no.
2 Use fair, responsible, and honest means to obtain information from people.
3 Treat your sources and the people you're writing about like the fellow human beings they are. Even if they allow you to share their words or views, think about who you are serving and who you might hurt. Invoke your own right, as the MEAA advises, "to resist compulsion to intrude".
4 Consider whether there is any reason for the people in your story to remain anonymous.
5 Share your draft with the people you're writing about, so they have an opportunity to correct any factual errors or raise any concerns.

Yourself

If your story isn't a personal one, you may be the last person on your mind. However, as an online writer, it is your name, your angle, and your words that will be accessible to the world as soon as you publish. Protecting yourself involves self-care, self-confidence, and resilience. These five tips offer some basic starting points for writer self-care.

1 **Take care of yourself while writing.** If you're writing about trauma or about a personal issue that may cause you distress, let a friend or colleague know. Call them if you need emotional support at any point and let them know when your story goes live.
2 **Think before you publish.** Ask yourself whether you're comfortable with your story being in the public eye. Don't publish anything that you'd be embarrassed or ashamed to watch on a national news report.
3 **Be prepared for criticism.** If you've fact checked and taken the time to write well, you should feel confident in what you've written. Sadly, this doesn't mean that everyone will appreciate your work. If your publishing platform allows comments, consider whether someone ought to approve them before they're made public.
4 **Be aware that the story may go viral.** As a result, you may receive a lot of unwanted attention – both positive and negative. Don't feel you need to acknowledge or reply to every comment, however supportive or vulnerable the person appears; you almost certainly don't have capacity for this.

If you find yourself a target for trolls, take screenshots of their actions and consider removing your story from the Internet. Replying to trolls or attempting to reason with them rarely improves the situation.

5 **Avoid revealing personally identifiable information.** If possible, protect your address and telephone number, and the names of your partner or children. If you're writing about a particularly contentious topic, consider publishing under a pseudonym.

Getting publication-ready

Before you hit "publish" or "post", you'll need to complete one final read-through and settle on the most attention-grabbing title.

Titles

Your title or headline acts like an advertisement for your story. It's displayed in search results, social media feeds, and the story itself. Titles combine with opening lines, visual designs, and any imagery to provide an at-a-glance offer to a potential reader or listener. Some platforms include an additional line of copy below the title. Known as a "standfirst", this summarises the story or clarifies its angle.

On social media, these elements attract readers or listeners by providing a glimpse of the story, a little like a trailer for a film. On the web, they provide information that helps search engines include your story in relevant search results. While a title should obviously reflect the content of a story, it ought to be written with search engines, and the reader or listener, in mind.

Your choice of title will be influenced by where you're publishing your story, how you expect your audience to find it and the terms prospective readers or listeners may type into search engines like Google. Known as keywords, these terms may be individual words or longer phrases.

In news stories, the headline usually communicates the essence of the story (so people don't need to read the whole article to find out what happened). In other situations, the title and standfirst may be crafted to arouse curiosity or to resonate with an audience's concerns and interests. While catchy titles in tune with the zeitgeist may gain attention in the short term, if you want your story to perform over time, avoid them. As Danny Birchall, Digital Manager at Wellcome Collection, says, "a cheeky headline could drive traffic on social, but a more accurate (if boring) one could bring a larger audience in the long-term".[17]

Though the algorithms that power search engines are complex and liable to change, if you want your content to be found online it's worth following these guidelines.

- Craft a unique title and standfirst, so your story stands out and your search result ranking rises.

- Include at least one relevant search engine optimisation (SEO) keyword, so people searching with this keyword have a chance of finding your story.
- Keep your title under 95 characters, and your standfirst under 250, so your copy can be read by search engines.
- Include any keywords, full names of people, places or events towards the start of the title or standfirst (in the first 160 characters), so search engines can find them.
- Be literal. Search engines aren't smart enough to decode metaphors or cryptic plays on words. If you're wedded to a clever pun in your title, make sure your standfirst or first line is direct and straightforward.

As an example of the many different ways of phrasing a title, let's imagine you've written a web-based story about Katherine Johnson, a NASA mathematician who played a key role in the Apollo Moon landings. As a starting point, ask yourself, "what will potential readers search for?" Would they use phrases like "Katherine Johnson" and "mathematician", "NASA", "Moon", or something else entirely? Your answer will depend on who your readers are and what interests them.

A quick way to identify potential keywords is to start typing within your browser bar and see what is suggested.[18] For instance, if you type "Katherine Johnson" into Google, the first suggestion is "Katherine Johnson story". That's a strong hint that you'll benefit if this term appears in your title or standfirst. With all this in mind, let's look at five options for introducing this story.

> **The Katherine Johnson story**
> *How mathematics helped NASA win the space race*

This descriptive title includes the keywords "Katherine Johnson story", "NASA", "mathematics", and "space race". It might work well for a reader who's aware of Johnson, but wants to know more about the mathematics.

> **Pioneering mathematician Katherine Johnson calculated flight paths for NASA astronauts**

Like a news headline, this stand-alone title informs us what Johnson did, while including "Katherine Johnson", "NASA", and "astronauts" as keywords. It might work well on social media, especially with people who haven't previously heard of Johnson.

> **Spacewoman**
> *How Katherine Johnson helped NASA shoot for the Moon*

This cryptic title is saved by a curiosity-raising standfirst, which includes "Katherine Johnson", "NASA", and "Moon". The combination might work well on social media, thanks to the attention-grabbing title.

> **Katherine Johnson's role in the space race**
> *The little-known NASA mathematician who calculated a route to the Moon*

This title and standfirst make it clear what the story is about, while including "Katherine Johnson", "mathematician", "space", "NASA", and "Moon". It's functional, so should work well with search engines. It may even fall into Danny Birchall's accurate-but-boring category: a title that will stand the test of time.

> **The hidden calculator**
> *The woman who guided Neil Armstrong to the Moon*

This cryptic title and descriptive standfirst includes the keywords "Neil Armstrong" and "Moon". It's the least satisfactory option, partly because it relies on the name of a male astronaut to gain attention for Johnson. More importantly, readers who land on the story wanting to know something about Armstrong's trip to the Moon may be disappointed to find a story about a mathematician.

With so many options, choosing a title can feel like an impossible task, which is why many online publications use A/B testing to try out alternatives. A/B testing involves publishing two almost identical versions of a story, where just one component differs. That component could be the title, the leading image or an aspect of the visual design. By publishing and promoting two versions of the story with different titles (e.g. on consecutive days) and monitoring their performance, you can identify which title delivers the greatest number of clickthroughs, web visits, or shares. The more titles you test, the more you'll learn about what works for your content and your readers and listeners.

Final checks

The final read (or listen) before you publish should ideally be performed when your text is in its final form (i.e. within a draft webpage or podcast file, in a social media preview or in a draft email). This gives you an opportunity to check that no errors have been introduced during editing and formatting, and that every component in your story (including the title and any images, audio, or video) combines to make a coherent and consistent whole.

At this stage, which is sometimes referred to as proofreading, your aim is to make as few changes as possible. If you've completed a thorough edit, you should have very little to worry out. Even so you ought to double-check:

1 Overall flow and clarity. Read the whole story to make sure everything is there, in the correct order, and that it makes sense.
2 Spellings of names, organisations, locations, specialist terms, and hashtags.
3 Consistency and adherence with the style guide (if there is one).
4 References, attributions, and credits (Are they all there? Are they formatted correctly?).
5 Hyperlinks (check that the URL is correct and that the link works).
6 Images (Are they reproduced at the appropriate size and resolution? Is any cropping appropriate?).
7 Formatting (Are headings, images, and lists in the correct format and appropriately aligned?).

For a final quick-and-dirty check for issues like lost full stops or missed italics read your story backwards. That way, you're not distracted by what words or sentences mean. This approach often reveals errors that you missed in every other manuscript read.

After you make any changes, step away. Keep revisiting your work and you'll always find something to improve. If your writing tells a story, is clear, accurate, and grammatically sound, it is fit for purpose. Congratulate yourself. Publish! Share on social media. And move on to your next story.

Summary

- Writing is such a cognitively demanding process that first drafts rarely make sense to readers and listeners. Inexperienced writers often underestimate the amount of time required for reviewing and revising their writing.
- However much we wish otherwise, our own unconscious biases may creep into our writing.
- Verifying evidence involves finding the original source, checking whether it's accurate, and considering why it may have been shared. Honest sources may provide inaccurate information thanks to flawed memories, missing context, or deliberate duping.
- In general, readers and listeners trust uncertain information less than certain information.

- Copyright automatically gives content creators the exclusive right to reproduce, distribute, adapt, or sell their own work. Reusing someone else's content without permission may be a copyright infringement, even if that material has been shared widely elsewhere.
- Your writing may appear anywhere online, including within the social media feeds of people who have not chosen to follow you.
- You have a duty of care to your readers and listeners, sources and subjects, and to yourself.

Practical lessons for online writers

- Recruit writing buddies, beta readers, or experts to provide fresh perspectives on your writing. Be prepared for honest, and potentially challenging, feedback.
- Read your first draft for story, inclusion, accuracy, clarity, and style, in each case advocating for your reader or listener. Work from a hard copy if you can.
- Prioritise structural changes before you deal with individual words. List out individual story events to help re-evaluate your structure.
- Look out for language that labels, language that judges, and language that excludes. Follow the reporting guidelines and codes of conduct published by national journalistic organisations.
- Look at every claim you make and ask yourself "How do I know that?" Double-check original sources, search for corroborating evidence, and document all the evidence you gather.
- To reduce the mistrust that comes from ambiguity, be open about your research process and try to pinpoint where uncertainty lies and why.
- Read your work aloud. This helps you spot long-winded phrases, changes of tone or pace, and passages that don't sound like you.
- Look for opportunities to cut material, while retaining meaning and flow.
- Consult style reference sources to help you make appropriate and consistent decisions about spelling and formatting.
- If you quote or share content from another source, always ask for permission from the copyright holder. If in doubt about copyright conditions, check with the copyright office in your country.
- Choose a title that reflects the content of your story, while taking your readers or listeners and the mechanics of SEO into account. Use A/B testing to evaluate the impact of different titles.

Recommended reading

Wynford Hicks, *English for Journalists, Twentieth Anniversary Edition* (Abingdon: Routledge, 2013) – accessible guide to journalistic writing, with a focus on grammar and style.

William Strunk and EB White, *The Elements of Style*, 4th edition (Needham Heights, MA: Allyn & Bacon, 2000) – classic and concise compendium of style tips for US writers.

Notes and references

1 Mark Kramer and Wendy Call, "Constructing a Structure Introduction", in *Telling True Stories: A Nonfiction Writers' Guide*, ed. Mark Kramer and Wendy Call (New York: Plume, 2007), pp. 97–8

2 Steven Pinker, *The Sense of Style: The Thinking Person's Guide to Writing in the 21st Century* (London: Penguin, 2014)

3 Anne Hull, "Revising – Over and Over Again", in *Telling True Stories: A Nonfiction Writers' Guide*, ed. Mark Kramer and Wendy Call (New York: Plume, 2007), pp. 205–8

4 You can assess your own unconscious bias by taking an implicit association test at <https://implicit.harvard.edu/implicit/takeatest.html>

5 Rebecca Solnit, *Whose Story is This? Old Conflicts, New Chapters* (London: Granta, 2019)

6 This example famously featured in a TV ad for the *Guardian* newspaper in 1986, which you can watch here: <https://www.youtube.com/watch?v=_SsccRkLLzU>

7 Full Fact, *Conspiracy Beliefs* <https://fullfact.org/media/uploads/en-conspiracy-beliefs.pdf> (accessed 3 May 2023)

8 American Press Institute, "Journalism as a Discipline of Verification" <https://www.americanpressinstitute.org/journalism-essentials/verification-accuracy/journalism-discipline-verification/> (accessed 5 June 2023)

9 For more on this, see Dora-Olivia Vicol, *How to Communicate Uncertainty*, Full Fact, Africa Check and Chequeado, October 2020 <https://fullfact.org/media/uploads/en-communicating-uncertainty.pdf> (accessed 28 November 2022)

10 Joseph M Williams, *Style: Ten Lessons in Clarity and Grace*, 5th edition (New York: Longman, 1997)

11 Rebecca McClanahan, "The Music of Sentences", in *Now Write! Nonfiction: Memoir, Journalism, and Creative Nonfiction Exercises from Today's Best Writers and Teachers*, ed. Sherry Ellis (New York: Jeremy P Tarcher / Penguin, 2009), pp. 218–22

12 Joseph M Williams, *Style*

13 Personal conversation with King Kurus, 19 December 2022

14 See <https://www.bbc.co.uk/newsstyleguide/> and https://www.govinfo.gov/collection/gpo-style-manual>

15 For instance, US authors should register their work with the US Copyright Office, as outlined here: <https://www.copyright.gov/circs/circ02.pdf>

16 For other international copyright offices, consult WIPO's directory at: <https://www.wipo.int/directory/en/urls.jsp>

17 Georgina Brooke, "Cultural Content with Danny Birchall: Wellcome Collection's Digital Content Manager Discusses Rolling Out Their 100th Story" *Cultural Content* newsletter, Substack, 11 May 2023 <https://culturalcontent.substack.com/p/cultural-content-with-danny-birchall> (accessed 11 May 2023)

18 Low-cost tools like keywordseverywhere.com can help you find appropriate keywords too.

Index

For Product Safety Concerns and Information please contact our EU representative GPSR@taylorandfrancis.com Taylor & Francis Verlag GmbH, Kaufingerstraße 24, 80331 München, Germany

Printed and bound by CPI Group (UK) Ltd, Croydon, CR0 4YY

08/06/2025

01897008-0020